Ron Jarvis

From Midland Compound

to the HST

by
John Chacksfield,
FBIS, AFAIAA, MRAeS, C.Eng

THE OAKWOOD PRESS

© Oakwood Press & John Chacksfield 2004

British Library Cataloguing in Publication Data
A Record for this book is available from the British Library
ISBN 0 85361 618 3

Typeset by Oakwood Graphics.
Repro by Ford Graphics, Ringwood, Hants.
Printed by Cambrian Printers, Aberystwyth, Ceredigion.

LMS 0-6-0 No. 17693, a Peter Drummond design of 1900 for the Highland Railway, but now with a Caledonian boiler, on the Strathpeffer train at Dingwall, 2nd August, 1933.
R.G. Jarvis Collection

Title page: No. 35022 *Holland America Line* prepared for service on the 'Bournemouth Belle'. *Jarvis Collection*

Front cover: LMS Compound 4-4-0 No. 1102 as depicted on a period picture postcard.
John Alsop Collection

Rear cover: A promotional postcard announcing the introduction of the HSTs on the Western Region. *Tony Harden Collection*

Published by The Oakwood Press (Usk), P.O. Box 13, Usk, Mon., NP15 1YS.
E-mail: oakwood-press@dial.pipex.com
Website: www.oakwood-press.dial.pipex.com

Contents

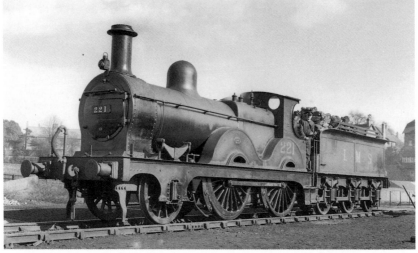

Ex-MR Johnson 2-4-0, built at Derby in 1880 as fitted with later Belpaire boiler. LMS No. 221 is found at Kettering shed 3rd March, 1934.   *R.G. Jarvis Collection*

Foreword

My brother Ron had hoped to write his own account of his interesting career on the railways, and he retained a quantity of reports and records for the purpose. Unfortunately he did not manage to start the book, initially because of the range of useful activities he undertook during retirement, followed by several years of distressing disability, which he bore with great fortitude and patience.

His store of technical records have been retained by his nephew by marriage, David Ward, and made available to the author for use in this excellent account of Ron's life, and to complement the wealth of personal reminiscences by family members and his colleagues during various stages of his career. Although he did not reach the heights he had always aimed for, he nevertheless had a significant influence on various matters in his own quiet, but persistent, way, and gained the respect of many of the leading railway engineering officers in this country and also on the Continent.

Most of his achievements have never been recorded for the public, apart from his name being widely associated with the rebuilding of the Bulleid Pacifics. Hence this book admirably fills the void, and describes his unique experiences with the gestation of the London, Midland & Scottish Railway (LMS) articulated 3-car diesel train; supervising the assembly of Stanier class '8F' 2-8-0s at Sivas on the wild Anatolian Highlands of Turkey; the arduous Machine Tool Mission to India in 1944 led by Sir William Stanier; together with plenty of more routine matters such as the design of several of the British Railways (BR) standard steam classes, plus electric and electro-diesel locomotives on the Southern Region, and finally the design of the mechanical parts of the prototype High Speed train (HST). Despite his lifelong interest in steam locomotives of all periods and pedigrees, he gave his full concentration to the development of newer forms of traction. He also strove hard for the preservation of really historic locomotives, drawings and photographs, etc., so it was natural for him to take on, virtually single-handed, his coach restoration projects for the Festiniog Railway.

Needless to say, he was a wonderful brother to me. Despite a 10 year age difference, he was always a real companion, whom I admired even as a toddler. Apart from his academic achievements, he was an outstanding craftsman with tools and instruments of all sorts. He encouraged me to share in his activities in model railways and photography, and patiently, but firmly, instructed me how to achieve higher quality in my handiwork as well as behaviour.

Whilst the story cannot be first-hand, the author has compiled an excellent review of Ron's life and career, which gives great satisfaction to our family and, hopefully, to the readers. I am delighted to have been invited by the author to write this Foreword.

J.M. (Jim) Jarvis
MSc (Illinois), C.Eng, MIMechE

Introduction and Acknowledgements

Behind every famous Chief Mechanical Engineer there was a team of first-class advisers/assistants, call them what you may. The work of these largely unsung persons was overseen and, where appropriate, adopted by their Chief in his continual drive to develop new stock to meet the ever-changing requirements as the railway scene moved through the advances in technology emanating from scientific progress in many relevant fields.

So often one finds the whole credit for such studies ends with the CMEs. They were well-known figures in the railway engineering scenario, and those persons actually responsible for the behind-the-scenes work were rarely credited with any commendation outside of the railway sphere. This book attempts to put this fact right in the context of the life and experiences of Ron Jarvis, who for many years was one of Stanier's team on the LMS and carried his expertise through into British Railways days at Brighton and Derby. The Brighton placing resulted in design leadership on the BR standard 2-6-4T, class '4' 4-6-0, the rebuilt Bulleid Pacifics and the design and developments of the class '9' 2-10-0, in addition to much work on electric, electro-diesel and diesel-electric designs. The Derby placing finishing on a high note with the design of power-car of the HST prototype. One feature of all designs attributed to Ron Jarvis was that they, almost without exception, were trouble-free from the start. They worked 'out of the box'. His meticulous attention to detail from the early days in their design saw to this.

When Jim Jarvis asked me to consider writing a biography of his brother, I immediately felt that here was an opportunity to bring one of the unsung into focus to rectify what I felt had been the neglect of a story on the lower rungs of the top engineering tasks ladder. A story capable of showing in some detail how the engineering aspects of railway matters were driven by teamwork from a small retinue of very skilled persons. After all, it was usually from these teams that the successors to the CMEs were found when retirement, or occasionally death, produced a post to be filled quickly by someone well versed in the workings of that high office.

I had actually begun collecting relevant data from my already extensive library of reference books and earlier writings. Ron Jarvis had already cropped up in my biography of Sir William Stanier and appeared to be a person who would be worth considering as a possible future subject. Jim's request, with the offer of much documentation collected by Ron whilst he was alive plus family archive material, closed the loop, and I felt that a worthwhile task awaited.

The story to be told covers a phase in railway history in which we will move from the four great grouped entities to the Nationalisation era. A time of transition to be viewed through the life and experiences of one who travelled that path and describing, through his eyes, the breadth of change as railways moved from the days of steam to the diesel and electric motive power with us now.

Undoubtedly, my first thanks must go to Jim for his request and his subsequent provision of extensive family data and personal recollections. Secondly, much information has been provided by Ron's nephew by marriage, David Ward, who has carefully preserved all the extensive documentation saved by Ron since his early days at Derby. There are several historic

Ron Jarvis in 1974.   *Jarvis Collection*

documents contained in this package, which enabled me to get an inside view of railway matters normally unavailable. One file of particular interest has been the detailed reports on the test programme on the abortive 'Leader' 0-6-6-0T of O.V.S. Bulleid, and a sizeable Chapter has been assigned to cover that episode of Ron's life.

I have also broken with my tradition of not including tables of runs in this particular book because, in the sorting out of data for the Chapter covering the development of the 3-car diesel set, I came across a report of an early test run from Derby to Gloucester and put this in to emphasise the advanced nature of this early attempt to provide a dmu on a British railway.

Others who have freely shared their reminiscences and information are D. Stewart Currie who met Ron in Egypt in 1947 when he was dispatched to select Stanier '8Fs' for repatriation; Brian Radford, who knew Ron in his final years at Derby and supplied much information and some crucial illustrations relevant to that time; Major W.W. Kirby, the onetime O.C. of 199 Railway Workshop in Jaffa; and last, but not least, Rosemary Boorne, Ron's daughter who kindly dug out many of his letters home during the overseas jaunts.

I have had a feast of photographs to choose from for this book, naturally many come from the collections of Ron and Jim Jarvis, from family archives and a splendid selection from Stewart Currie covering the Egyptian episode. Many of the Jarvis collection are photographs of great historic interest and are published in this book for the first time, for Ron travelled extensively at every opportunity to build up a superb selection of British, Irish and Continental locomotive portraits worth recording.

Great Southern Railway (Ireland) 2-2-2WT No. 483, a Fairbairn product of 1855, is still in service at Waterford in 1935 on the Waterford and Tramore branch. Sadly, a week after this photograph was taken this historic engine was on a train derailed by vandals and cut up for scrap, even though it had been earmarked for preservation. *R.G. Jarvis Collection*

Harpenden High Street as it would have looked during Ron's boyhood days.   *Jarvis Collection*

'Glendale', Moreton Avenue, the first family home in Harpenden. This was one of the first of many quality homes built by Ernest Jarvis' company.   *Jarvis Collection*

Chapter One

The Early Years

The year 1905 was one in which the Liberal landslide victory was to be the beginning of the end for that party's governmental prowess, despite their 377 seats which gave them a comfortable majority of 84 over the combined opposition of the Unionists, Irish Nationalists and Labour parties. Overseas the Union of South Africa, which grew out of the wreckage of the Boer War, was two years from the first foundation of fully responsible government so much sought after by Rhodes. A minor, but important, event in the Home Counties was when Ernest Charles Jarvis, from Enfield, realised an ambition and set up his own building business at Harpenden, a business which flourishes to this day. This had been brought about by a suggestion from his elder brother, Joseph John (later Sir John), who was working in the family firm J. Jarvis & Sons, which was participating in the building of a new Post Office in Harpenden. The suggestion was that Harpenden would appear to be a promising place to set up a new building business. Ernest duly cycled over from Enfield to size up the situation, was suitably impressed, and started setting up his company. Legend has it that at least one local builder remarked that this upstart would not last long!

The stability soon engendered by Ernest's enterprise led him into married life with Phoebe Edith Mockridge whose father had his own engineering company at Plaistow in East London. The wedding took place at Clapton Church, London on 26th July, 1906. Initially, the newly-weds lived at 'Glendale', Moreton Avenue, one of a batch of houses built by Ernest's company. In 1909 their first son, Geoffrey, who was to follow his father and join the family business, was born. Two years later, on 5th November, their second son, Ronald Guy (Ron), our subject, arrived. The choice of the new arrival's second name was prompted by the date of his birth. The family was later completed by a daughter, Heather, born in 1916 and a third and final son, James (Jim) in 1922.

Harpenden lay on the Midland Railway (MR) main line from St Pancras to the Midlands and Ron's first sight of steam locomotives probably included early Compounds on express duties, Kirtley and Johnson 0-6-0s on freight tasks interspersed with Deeley 0-6-4 tanks hauling commuter traffic.

The building business clearly flourished as World War I approached, for Ernest Jarvis became the second person in Harpenden to own a motor car, the first having been the local doctor. With this company and the engineering concern of Ron's maternal grandparents, construction in various forms was clearly in the family blood.

Childhood days were happy ones, the family was closely-knit and had similar abilities, personalities and interests. Ron remembered those days fondly, when despite the onset of the Great War, matters at home ran smoothly and efficiently. One of his earliest recollections of his life involved being ushered out of the house to watch the death throes of a Zeppelin as it fell as a flaming wreck near Cuffley to the south-east. He also remembered that a family friend,

The Jarvis family at Harpenden in 1913. Ron on his mother's lap next to dog; brother Geoffrey to left of dog.   *Jarvis Collection*

1914 finds Geoffrey and Ron enjoying the delights of a sandpit.   *Jarvis Collection*

The first car with the family as in 1914.   *Jarvis Collection*

Schoolboys now, Ron and Geoffrey, pose for an official photograph in 1920.   *Jarvis Collection*

By 1920, the family had expanded, with sister Heather now around.   *Jarvis Collection*

Bernard Smart, ranked amongst the first airmen to shoot down a Zeppelin, over the North Sea, not an easy task in the aircraft of the day, with their limited performance at the altitudes maintained by the large, but very explosive, target.

Another childhood experience recalled was of being taken with his elder brother to Paddington to see the Great Western Railway (GWR) publicity piece, the one and only Pacific in the UK, *The Great Bear*. Unfortunately they did not see that, but Ron remembered a 'County' class 4-4-0, which despite being much smaller, to him seemed enormous. The example in question was No. 3829 *County of Merioneth*.

In 1920, his parents deposited the two boys, Geoff and Ron, as short-term boarders at St George's School and Heather with relatives in order to travel to Canada for a fact-finding trip. With the war over and the situation in England none too stable Ernest Jarvis wished to sound out the possibilities of settling in Canada and taking advantage of the recent boom in business there.

They sailed across the Atlantic and up the St Lawrence to Montreal where they boarded a train for the journey across the continent to Vancouver. *En route* they visited Ottawa, Toronto, Winnipeg, Edmonton and Calgary before crossing the Rockies on the Canadian Pacific Railway. One place at which they made a brief stay, Harrison Hotsprings, nearly proved to be a catastrophe as the hotel in which they were staying caught fire and was burned to the ground. Ernest was alerted in time and managed to throw their bags out of the window to safety. Following this event the trip was rounded off by a voyage up the inland passage to Skagway and then on the White Pass & Yukon Railway to Whitehorse, where they travelled by old stern-wheeler to Dawson deep in Yukon Territory. The opportunities in Canada seeming to be over, plans for emigration of the family were cancelled and they returned home to Harpenden to continue life there.

St George's School, Harpenden.   *J.M. Jarvis*

The School gymnastic team. Ron in front of Sgt Munday.

Jarvis Collection

Following the abortive trip to Canada, the building business continued to prosper and, in 1922, a move of home within Harpenden resulted. The new house, 'Gorselands', and the associated outbuildings, stood in some three acres of grounds encompassing woods, extensive lawns, an orchard and a splendid grass tennis court. At the bottom of these grounds lay the Midland main line, on a high embankment leading to the well-known skew bridge in South Harpenden. This move delighted Ron, as by now trains had become quite a passion, with both the real thing and models an important feature of his spare time. The latter aspect took on more importance after the 'Gorselands'move, as there was a large playroom where he set up his extensive gauge '0' tinplate track, and began a life-long interest in making and operating his model trains. The railway interest really took off and is illustrated by the fact that Ron, shortly after the move, cycled alone all the way to Welwyn in the hope of seeing one of Gresley's new pair of magnificent Pacifics. In fact, he was incredibly lucky and managed to see both of them on prestige express trains that one day, although he had considerable difficulty in getting his mother to believe this!

One day brother Jim, when no more two or three, was permitted to go into the playroom, but unfortunately his nanny allowed him to touch one of the engines resting on a table. This particular one had, shortly before, been repainted and was not yet dry, so Jim's attention resulted in some smudges and a strong complaint from Ron about the nanny's decision!

Other features of this new home, apart from the air of spaciousness, was a full-size billiard table in the house and an outbuilding containing a large room initially used for table tennis, parties and, later, dances. Electricity for the home was supplied by an engine-driven generator set located in an outhouse. The supply was 50 volts and served the family well until the early 1930s when mains electricity from the new National Grid became available. Despite all these assets and the not inconsiderable wealth, extravagance was not on the agenda, and expenditure was carefully controlled by all.

The children's education was served by the local co-educational St George's School at Harpenden, a predominantly boarding establishment which they attended as day pupils. Ron often cycled to school and recalled one incident of having his bicycle confiscated, along with those of several other pupils, by the House Master, the crime being that they were not padlocked as required by the School rules. His sense of injustice welled up, and with the support of most of the other boys, he hired the stately horse-drawn cab, which was often to be found at the railway station, to convey them to school on Speech Day, which was imminent. Some of his colleagues chickened out before the cab reached the school. When it did, the House Master marched out to greet the anticipated eminent personality only to find some of his pupils alighting! Fortunately he saw the funny side of this prank and promptly returned the bicycles to their owners!

Summer holidays were sometimes spent in North Wales, at Barmouth, the house used being near the railway station. These holidays produced the opportunity for the boys to study the locomotives fussing around shunting the small yard which lay behind their abode. Ron recalled this in later years when talking about his early impressions of such viewings which clearly had such an

One of the earliest surviving photographs taken by Ron Jarvis (in 1926). This shows the incline and tunnel down to the harbour at Newquay.   *R.G. Jarvis*

'Gorselands', East Common, Harpenden.   *J.M. Jarvis*

impact on his choice of railway engineering as a career. The best view could be had from the most important room in the house and he recalled being ticked off several times for his extensive occupancy of this! The railway bug had now taken root, for in 1923, when he was 11, he was awarded a prize at school. On being asked what book he would like to receive, he immediately replied, 'A railway book'. 'Oh, no', came the reply, 'That is only a passing interest'. 'Oh no', replied Ron, 'I am going to work on the railway'. Doubtless the teachers thought he had the usual small boy's wish to be an engine driver, but he got his railway book. It was endorsed: 'Awarded to R.G. Jarvis for reaching the award standard in: 'An Essay on Railways, Railway Models and the commendation standard in Drawing and Physical Training'.'

His railway modelling now becoming an increasingly important interest, Ron took advantage of the many opportunities presented by 'Gorselands'. A large loft extended over the garage near to the house and had an adjacent harness room which he was turning into a workshop. This loft was entered by a narrow wooden staircase and before long he and his elder brother were assembling timber trestles upon which were laid battens to carry the over-scale steel track of the day. The stock of commercial clockwork engines accumulated and Ron began, in the workshop, to construct various coaches and wagons, followed by his first scratch-built engine, a London & North Western Railway (LNWR) 2-4-2 tank. Some old basic 0-4-0 tanks were also rebuilt into more representative machines. The primary interest was in the construction of the stock and here we see the awakening of what was to become a career at the ultimate scale of 12 inches to the foot!

In 1925 the Jarvis family visited the Empire Exhibition at Wembley, at which were displayed two classic locomotives, the GWR *Caerphilly Castle* of Collett and the London & North Eastern Railway's (LNER) Gresley Pacific *Flying Scotsman*. Jim, although only a toddler at the time, clearly recalls Ron leapfrogging a row of silver posts and the enormity of the locomotives, gleaming and polished, on their display stands.

Ron's progress at school was excellent, which boded well for the future, and he had gained his school certificate and matriculation exemption when he was fifteen. His sporting prowess was never great, but being lightly built, he made his mark as a gymnast in the team trained by Sergeant Munday. Being quite agile and light he usually ended up as the top of the pyramid in displays. By now the determination to adopt engineering as a career was firmly in his mind and, against the wishes of the Headmaster, he left school in 1927 and spent a short time in the family engineering firm at Plaistow before going, with brother Geoffrey, to France for a few months. Here they stayed with the family of M. Joubert, the HM Consular Agent in Lorient, Brittany, to improve their French and doubtless taking an interest in the French railway scene. About a year later M. Joubert's son, Henri, had a return visit to 'Gorselands'.

The start for Ron of what was to be a lifelong interest in photography began in the mid-1920s when he acquired a small roll-film camera. Use of this was made to record family events, holidays and, of course, the current railway scene. As the interest grew a new camera, taking a 120 size film, replaced the original. This hobby was given extra interest by one of Ron's boyhood friends,

John Adams, who was to become a professional photographer well-known for his railway pictures. Their association was to last a lifetime.

Geoffrey had already joined the family building firm, and Ron had decided that the railways were for him. Accordingly, his father applied on his behalf for a privileged apprenticeship at the Derby locomotive works of the LMS. The two of them were called for interview with a Mr G.W. Woolliscroft whose duties had been the Superintendent of Apprentices at Derby since Midland Railway days in 1908, prior to which he had held various positions in the locomotive drawing office. At the turn of the century, he had acted as a design office liaison man for the then Locomotive Superintendent, S.W. Johnson. Any time Johnson was discussing locomotive developments with the Directors of the Midland Railway, he had Woolliscroft with him for consultation on details under discussion. When Johnson sent R.M. Deeley to the USA he ordered Woolliscroft to accompany him. On that trip Woolliscroft, due to his affability and talkative manner, grabbed most of the attention. Later, when Deeley became Locomotive Superintendent, he put Woolliscroft 'under the table', with a sideways move to Superintendent of Apprentices. The interview was held in the splendour of the Great Hall at Euston station. Ron took with him a home-made model of a brake van and was horror-struck when his father made a present of it to Mr Woolliscroft.

Around the time his elder brother was settling into the family business, Ron and his father departed to Paris for a few days. Their mode of travel was not the popular train-boat-train journey but involved a flight by Imperial Airways from Croydon Airport. Air travel was still very much a novelty in those days, the aeroplanes in use being multi-engined biplanes with cruising speeds barely in excess of 100 mph. Doubtless his recently brushed up French was put to good use in and around Paris.

Air travel in the 1920s was a luxury open to a few, and somewhat basic compared to today. This view was taken at Le Bourget on the Paris trip of 1928.   *Jarvis Collection*

Ron was eventually accepted for his apprenticeship and, in October 1928, his parents drove him up to Derby and installed him in digs for the commencement of his career on the railways.

Just before Ron departed for Derby the photographic interest was enlivened by the appearance of brightly painted new Fowler 2-6-4Ts which were beginning to replace the 0-6-4Ts on some surburban services. Also the first of the massive Garratts appeared on the lengthy coal trains which, up to now, had been double-headed by 0-6-0s of various vintages, from double-framed Kirtleys to the Fowler '4F' class.

Reporting at the works for the start of his time there, Ron's first posting was to the iron foundry, at the eastern extremity of the site. The hours were long, weekdays 7.55 am to 5.30 pm with an hour for lunch, plus 7.55 am to 12.00 noon on Saturdays. However, for most of his apprenticeship the Saturday shift was off, owing to the difficult financial situation of the railways at that time. Being of slight build, the early tasks allotted him of shovelling sand into the massive moulds were sometimes exhausting. One day, seeing he was tiring, the moulder nearby remarked to his mate, 'Look, the poor lad's booggered!'

Privileged apprentices were a cut above the other apprentices in that they could obtain special dispensation for extra leave on special occasions. This happened for Ron at Easter 1929 when his father obtained three passages from London to Marseilles on the P&O RMS *Viceroy of India* liner's maiden voyage for Ron, Geoffrey and himself. Obtaining the cabins was not too difficult for the early part of the voyage to the Far East, as many passengers making the full journey would have travelled overland to join the vessel at Marseilles. So, on Thursday 27th March Ron, Geoffrey and their father left Harpenden on the 9.50 am and changed at St Pancras for the boat train to Tilbury. At 4.30 pm they sailed down the Thames towards the open sea. Good Friday passed as they sailed down the Channel towards the Bay of Biscay, which was smooth. Easter Sunday, as they sailed on down the coast of Portugal, began with a ship's service, conducted by the chaplain and the Bishop of Worcester.

Gibraltar was reached early on 1st April and the ship steered into the anchorage offshore, which was crowded with capital ships of the Royal Navy. The HM warships *London, Marlborough, Rodney, Resolution, Royal Oak, Revenge* and *Royal Sovereign* all swung at anchor on the starboard side and on the port side were the aircraft carriers *Courageous, Furious* and *Argus*.

Ron, Geoff and their father disembarked on the first shore tender to visit the town of Gibraltar. In the inner harbour they saw more Naval ships, the *Queen Elizabeth, Nelson, Hood* and *Frobisher*, so it seemed that most of the home fleet was in port. After a brief tour of the town they took a paddle steamer to Algeciras where Ron quickly located the railway station where there was a sizeable locomotive shed. The locomotives in sight ranged from some Belgian-built 2-6-0s of 1885 to 4-4-0s and 2-6-0s built by Beyer, Peacock in 1890. Following this there was just time for tea at a nearby hotel before returning to Gibraltar and catching the last tender for their boat.

At 9.30 am the next day the *Viceroy of India* set sail for the South of France. Towards the end of the second day, as they neared land, the 'Mistral' began to blow. By late evening the ship was being battered by the short, sharp waves

Right: P&O *Viceroy of India* at Gibraltar, 1929.   *R.G. Jarvis*

Below: HMS *Revenge* at Gibraltar, 1929.   *R.G. Jarvis*

A large number of the Home Fleet at Gibraltar, as caught by Ron's camera.   *R.G. Jarvis*

This old RENFE 4-4-0 was found at Alicante in 1967. One of a class of four built by Beyer, Peacock in 1891 it is seen here withdrawn and stored for preservation and could be the type spotted by Ron in 1929.   *J.M. Jarvis*

associated with the wind and it was not long before some portholes on the starboard side were smashed in. Through the rest of the night the storm continued until Marseilles was sighted. The next few hours were spent manoeuvring to get into the port. It took no fewer than eight tugs to control matters and get the vessel alongside the quay and the gangways placed. Then as suddenly as it had appeared, the wind abated and they were able to go ashore and make arrangements for their onward journey through France the next day. They slept aboard for the final night and disembarked to begin a week's tour of the Riviera and Southern France.

The tour took them to Nice, Monte Carlo, Menton, Digne, and Grenoble where, after a night stop, they entrained for Paris on the 10.00 pm departure, sleeping on the train. Paris reached, they changed to the Gare du Nord and boarded the 10.00 am for Calais to embark on the Southern Railway's *Maid of Kent* for Dover.

Dover to Harpenden was via Victoria and St Pancras and they arrived home from a fascinating journey at 9.50 pm on Saturday 13th April. The following day Ron was on his way back to Derby and his apprenticeship tasks in the works.

The *Viceroy of India* was the first turbo-electric vessel built for the P&O line and was unique in that she had the first indoor swimming pool to be found on an ocean liner. World War II claimed her as one of its victims during the Allied landings in North Africa, where she was torpedoed in November 1942.

Ron and his father in the South of France, having put ashore at Marseilles for the return to the UK.   *J.M. Jarvis*

A typical early LMS scene, still plenty of double-heading around. This is the morning train to Derby at Harpenden. Ron is leaning out of the window in the leading coach door.
J.M. Jarvis

As time went on, moves to the machine, boiler, boiler mounting and erecting shops took place to ensure that his practical experience was broadly based. The works were busy in the early apprenticeship years, as the 0-6-0 dock tanks and final batch of the class '2P' 4-4-0s were turned out, followed by 75 of the Fowler 2-6-4Ts, batches of 2-6-2Ts, 20 'Royal Scots' and the prototype 'Patriots' or 'Baby Scots'. On top of all this new construction, as with all railway works, a major part of the works' activities involved the maintenance of the existing fleet of locomotives. Additionally there was a steady trickle of old types coming in for scrapping, in particular some ancient Kirtley double-framed 0-6-0s.

Following its catastrophic water tube burst, the experimental high-pressure boilered 4-6-0 *Fury* arrived at Derby, and a fitter and Ron were sent to help a Frank Pepper in making some modification to cab equipment. Pepper was from the drawing office and had been the draughtsman from the experimental section involved in the trials in Scotland and had experienced the burst whilst on the footplate, but had fortunately escaped injury. The Superheater Company's representative and the fireman had both been seriously injured and the former had died as a result of this mishap. In fact the locomotive only underwent sporadic steaming after repair and was stored until a rebuild by Stanier in 1935.

One of the fitters whom Ron encountered was, one day, trying to explain the mysteries of brake systems to another apprentice and was overheard to mention that the reservoir in question contained compressed vacuum!

Having first seen the Kirtley double-framed designs in service on the Midland main line at Harpenden in his schoolboy days, Ron was resigned to the fact that these classic locomotives were rapidly approaching extinction by the time his apprenticeship commenced, for they were arriving by the dozen for scrapping. However, he managed to photograph many of them. There were the odd exceptions around as indicated in a letter written in 1978 concerning historic locomotives:

Metropolitan Railway No. 23 on the Brill branch train at Quainton Road, 6th June, 1933. The coach at the rear is a rigid 8-wheel type. *R.G. Jarvis*

This ex-North Staffs Railway 2-4-2T was caught at Burton shed on 5th July, 1933. *R.G. Jarvis*

I recall, during my apprenticeship in the Loco Works, 1928-1932, one of my contemporary 'Privs' coming into nine shop with the news that No. 60 had arrived at Deadman's Lane. I was incredulous, believing all the '800' class to have been broken up. Oh yes, it's a double-framed 2-4-0, ever so black and dirty - looks as though it hasn't been through the Works for years. It hadn't. Somehow one of the class had managed to carry on working quietly, at Westhouses I think, and contrived thereby to outlive all its sisters by a considerable number of years to become No. 20060. She went to Peterborough for a while and there joined another last survivor, No. 311, a 7 ft 4-4-0 with a 'B' class boiler.

No. 60, or 20060 as it was then, had been built in April 1870 to Kirtley's design and later rebuilt by Johnson in 1876. This class was at one time reckoned as being the finest design of express locomotive turned out in the Kirtley era.

For some of the apprentices, footplate trips were an occasional and sometimes pleasurable diversion from the normal tasks allotted them in the works. One such trip enjoyed by Ron, on 18th January, 1932, was on Compound No. 1104 during express runs between Derby and St Pancras. This locomotive was one of the 1925 batch of 30 Compounds which introduced the recently decreed LMS standard left-hand driving position to that class. The trials were in connection with the installation of non-standard superheater elements of one inch diameter. His task on these runs was to note the readings at intervals of steam and smokebox temperatures plus boiler and receiver pressures, regulator and reverser positions. The trains involved were the 9.40 am Derby to St Pancras with a return on the 2.25 pm from St Pancras. The loads were quite moderate, 140 tons increased to 241 tons at Nottingham on the up run and 319 tons on the down run. The driver was C. Tatman from Derby. Ron was able to let the family know the time of the trains involved, so that his brothers could wave to him from the footbridge at Harpenden as they sped through.

Several other trips were also made on this engine, some of them through to Manchester over the Peak District on a very spectacular section of the main line. One run was notable for what could have been a catastrophic event, in Ron's own words, 'Mercifully no one was in line with the firehole, for this example of a blowback had been known to be fatal':

In Monsal Dale there was a long rock cutting with sharp curves, interspersed with ledges from which the valley could be seen below. Then there was a viaduct, at the south end of which the track plunged into Monsal Head tunnel. My first experience on an express locomotive on this line was terrifying. The moment we were over the viaduct, steam had been shut off and we plunged into the tunnel. The engine rolled violently in the pitch blackness and then a huge flame licked out of the firehole, passed through the cab and right over the tender, scorching the paintwork of the leading coach. The heat of it caused us all to shield our faces with our hands. By the grace of God I was standing at the cabside hanging on to the rails like grim death.

One of Ron's apprenticeship colleagues, a Patrick Jaekel, had a further task allotted him on the cross-country run from Bristol to Birmingham, again on a Compound. This entailed descending beneath the engine at each stop and taking the readings of some clearances near the front bogie. At one stop, the crew changed, with those leaving the engine failing to tell the new crew of Jaekel's position. At the right away, the driver opened the regulator to start off. Jaekel was alerted to his action by a leak of steam from the high pressure

An old 2-4-0, No. 60, at Derby works after a general repair, *c.*1930.   *R.G. Jarvis Collection*

On a trip to North Wales in 1930, Ron took this picture of the remains of single Fairlie 0-4-4T *Taliesin* at Boston Lodge works, little knowing that he would be heavily involved on the Festiniog Railway in later years.   *R.G. Jarvis Collection*

cylinder gland and threw himself down on the track. Unfortunately, his overalls caught on something resulting in his being dragged along for some distance as the train accelerated. Eventually, the top half of the overalls tore away, leaving him lying on the sleepers. Suddenly, someone, somewhere realised that he was still underneath and the train came to an emergency stop, by which time some four coaches had passed over where he lay. A very shaken, but intact, Jaekel clambered out from under the train, resulting in some ladies fainting at the sight of this bedraggled figure appearing, minus the top half of his clothing. Given a few minutes to clean himself up and borrow a fresh pair of overalls, Jaekel remounted the footplate and set off to finish his task. The driver's comments on this event were, it is believed, quite unprintable!

During the end of his apprenticeship Ron had a spell in the running shed, and among other duties, was a member of the breakdown gang. This entailed being called out at night by the 'knocker up' when derailments occurred. He recalled spending one particularly cold, wet, night at Tamworth High Level station, where a Garratt locomotive and 13 wagons had been derailed between the platforms.

As a privileged apprentice, later to be re-named engineering apprentice, he had day release to attend Derby Technical College. Initially, this was without pay. This 'day release' actually consisted of two mornings a week. He also attended evening classes on three or four evenings a week. After the college evening attendances came homework which usually kept him busy until midnight and often into the small hours. Friday nights were kept free, for with no Saturday shift, that was the time for him to travel home. Later, when studying for the Finals, he used to go to Nottingham University on Saturday mornings for extra classes. Life was certainly hard but it enabled him to take the London External B.Sc. Engineering Degree, in which he obtained a Second Class Honours pass, in addition to the standard Higher National Certificate awarded at Derby Tech. He found the practical work in the works during the day and theoretical studies at college were a good foil for one another, as learning about the things he was handling in the works made retention in the memory much easier.

The jobs in the works for a 'Privileged' were the same as those for a trade apprentice, often filthy and sometimes quite menial. The pay was quite moderate - in fact his first pay packets contained 6s. 6d. This was just sufficient for his concessionary (¼ fare) return ticket home to Harpenden each weekend. For his personal expenses, food, digs, etc., his father gave him a weekly allowance, which just covered them.

During his first year in the works he applied to compete for the Directors Prize, but was told that it was too soon and he had little or no chance of achieving it. This only made him persist, and he asked if he could see some previous papers for guidance, a request which met with the comment that this was unfair, even though others after this prestigious award repeatedly took the exam and were familiar with the content. Eventually, his persistence won and permission to enter was granted. The cynics were confounded when he came top and was awarded the prize. The keen engineering expertise was beginning to show. Expertise, which allied to a strong desire to get as high as possible up the ladder to a top job, was to benefit the British railway motive power scenario considerably.

Derby No. 8 erecting shop August 1929

J.M. Jarvis Collection

Chapter Two

From Derby to Euston and Back

In those days, apprenticeship ended upon reaching one's 21st birthday. By the time this came along Ron was in the works drawing office, where he was given the task of examining articles of an engineering nature which had been damaged in transit, assessing if possible the causes and suggesting methods of avoiding damage in further shipments.

On completion of his apprenticeship, Ron was offered a draughtsman's position in the Locomotive Drawing Office (LDO) in London Road, Derby. Although this offered an opening to the design side of things, what he had hoped for had been a works placing, as the CME's positions were, it seemed, generally filled by Works Managers. Ron had, from those early days, an ambition to try and attain that high position. In fact, his answer to Sir Henry Fowler's query on his ultimate position he intended to aim for on the railway was, 'Yours, Sir', asked at his only meeting with that eminent CME early in his apprenticeship. However, he accepted the LDO placing and started his professional career at a time of change in the CME's Department as W.A. Stanier, the new CME, began to implement his authority from Euston.

In 1933, shortly after his apprenticeship drew to a close, Ron acquired his first car. This was his mother's old Austin Seven which she was discarding having bought a new one. Having a car gave Ron much more opportunity to make diversions to photograph unusual railway scenes when driving home and, of course, during holiday weekends. Many times he had the company of John Adams and Frank Carrier with their cameras on the latter jaunts. Also, from about 1935, Jim also accompanied them and was instructed on the use of the camera. This book contains a large number of Jarvis (both Jim and Ron) photographs as a result.

By the middle of 1933 the Derby LDO had completed the detail design of the first Stanier Pacific of which two prototypes were being built at Crewe. The draughtsmen were also busy in scheming the revised taper boiler 3-cylinder 4-6-0, based on the Fowler rebuild of the 'Claughton', which was to become the 'Jubilee' class. The Stanier 2-6-0 was being dealt with by the design office at Horwich under Coleman. Stanier had the task of bringing the locomotive fleet of the LMS up-to-date and had implemented his 'scrap-and-build' programme. So there was certainly plenty of work for all the staff of the LDO at this time.

On top of all the effort at Derby, Ron still wished to gather more qualifications under his belt and embarked on a course of study at Nottingham University, under Professor Bulleid, to enable him to obtain the corporate membership of the Institution of Mechanical Engineers. Additionally, he also lectured at Derby Technical College on a part-time, evening, basis, his subject being engineering drawing.

One of Ron's colleagues in the LDO was a Frank Carrier, a draughtsman engaged on the diesel-hydraulic shunter project which was then current. Carrier was a fine, quick, worker with a good brain and also a very good railwayman. The factor which drew them together was their mutual interest in photography. He was also somewhat of an expert in the use of a bulky reflex

No. 8 shop again in 1933, with the last batch of Fowler 2-6-4Ts under construction.
J.M. Jarvis Collection

A small-boilered 'Claughton' prepares to leave St Pancras with an express in 1929.
R.G. Jarvis Collection

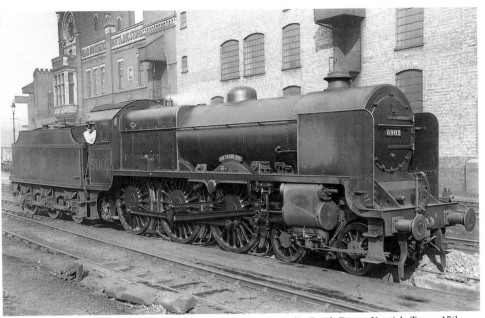

One of the two original 'Claughton' rebuilds, No. 5902 *Sir Frank Ree* at Kentish Town 15th October, 1933.
R.G. Jarvis Collection

Ex-LNWR 'Prince of Wales' 4-6-0 No. 25797 at Bletchley shed 15th June, 1938.
R.G. Jarvis Collection

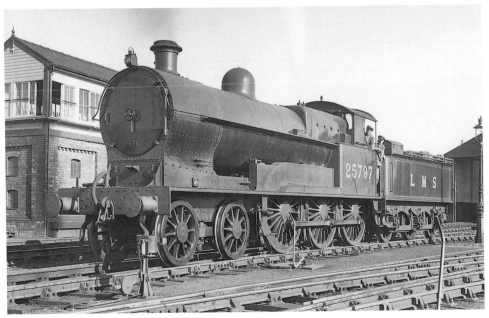

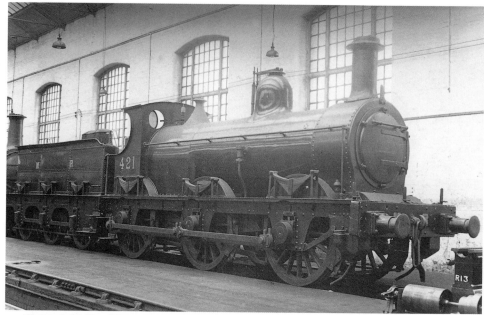

Kirtley 0-6-0 No. 421, as preserved in Derby paint shop when Ron arrived as an apprentice; sadly cut up on the orders of Stanier in 1933.   *R.G. Jarvis Collection*

Another relic from the past, this 2-4-0 No. 156a was also cut up in 1933.   *R.G. Jarvis Collection*

plate camera of 4¼ inch by 3¼ inch format. Many of Carrier's photos impressed Ron and he decided to use a plate camera himself. The first such camera, being a folding bellows type, was less bulky to carry around. Later, in 1936 he found a second-hand Goertz Tenax with a first-class Dagor lens. It was in almost mint condition and Ron purchased it for a relatively small sum. It did have one slight disadvantage, however, this being the fact that it only came with a few plate carriers of an obsolete type. Ron put his engineering expertise to work and a few hours spare time effort altered the camera to take the available standard holders. The old camera was put on one side and all photography now took place with the new acquisition, which was passed to his brother Jim in 1938 and used by him for some 20 more years. In fact, it still exists and is in working order, but unfortunately glass plates are no longer available.

Just before Sir Henry Fowler had retired from the LMS in 1932 he had commenced to set up a Research Department at Derby. In 1934 this was expanded under the direction of Sir Harold Hartley, a Vice-President and Director of Scientific Research. A new building was erected for this department in London Road, adjacent to the LDO, and opened in that year. The staffing was largely made up by transfers from the existing engineering departments plus sundry other specialists injected by Hartley. Ron was one offered a position in this new office and settled in to expand his experience in the research area. This placing entailed his being put onto the permanent staff at the salary of £200 per year. His responsibilities were in the design of special types of testing machines and equipment. He learned a lot in his time there, but he still hankered after higher things.

One particular task which came his way in Research was to assist in the design of a large 'Wohler' type rotating bending machine to investigate the fatigue of axles which had press-fitted wheels. There were an increasing number of carriage axles which were found cracked or which broke in service; this latter occurrence thankfully being infrequent as they could result in a dangerous derailment. After much testing on this machine it was discovered that a simple change of dimension and geometry where the wheel fitted the axle would give a considerable improvement to the strength of the assembly, but by then Ron was based at the CME's Department in Euston.

On the weekends back at home in Harpenden, Ron still indulged in his railway modelling and by now had handed on to Jim the older, redundant, stock and track as the more correct finer scale layout in the loft over the garage was updated. Some of Jim's practices, such as temporarily laying out the track in the garden, were initially frowned upon but eventually accepted.

The old Austin Seven was disposed of in late 1934 to be replaced with a second-hand Standard 'Swallow'. This had an aluminium body which eliminated rust problems and was to serve Ron for over 20 years. This car was to feature in many holiday jaunts. In 1935, it was shipped over to Ireland for a touring holiday from Larne to Rosslare, the journey taking Geoffrey, Ron, Jim and Heather along the Antrim Coast Road to Londonderry, into Donegal, down the West Coast and across via Cork to Rosslare. Two years later it was ferried across to Oslo in Norway for an extensive tour of that country and Western Sweden, returning via Stavanger. Overseas trips with cars were a rarity in those days, with the vehicles being hoisted aboard the ships by cranes.

Ron's Standard 'Swallow' bought in 1934 and used for nearly 20 years. Many journeys were made in this car both at home and overseas in the quest for photographs of historic locomotives.
R.G. Jarvis

Easter 1936 found (*left to right*) Frank Carrier, John Adams, Ron and Jim Jarvis in South Wales on a trip to photograph yet more trains. This shot was taken by delayed action on Carrier's camera, hence his rather apprehensive look.   *Jarvis Collection*

The photographic trips at home were many and varied, sometimes Ron departing on his own and at other times in the company of Frank Carrier and John Adams, and later with young brother Jim as well. Carrier, in the mid-1930s, decided that carrying around a large and heavy reflex plate camera was a bit exhausting and invested in a roll-film camera. The glass plates themselves were heavy and the need to change them in the plate holders after a day's photography could be a bit of a problem. Usually this took place after dark in a sheltered drawer; possibly under the bed-clothes; occasionally down in a cellar, and quite often inside a wardrobe. This last method had its hazards, as Adams found, when in the middle of proceedings, the wardrobe capsized and trapped its door against the bedpost! Assistance took some time to be organised as Carrier, who was in the room at the time, was doubled up with laughter.

Permission to visit railway and industrial sites for the photography was never too difficult to obtain and they were given leave to wander around searching for subjects. Being railwaymen themselves doubtless helped matters.

As Ron started his Research time at Derby the locomotives now running from St Pancras would have included the odd ex-LNWR 'Claughton' and 'Prince of Wales' 4-6-0s as they were displaced by the 'Royal Scots' at Euston. Although the Compounds were to remain the mainstay of motive power on the old MR route until the mid-1930s. His journeys to and from Harpenden were often behind Compounds, although these moderately sized locomotives were often double-headed in typical Midland fashion until 'Jubilees' and 'Black Fives' appeared in quantity. The old MR legacy took a relatively long time to die away.

Clearly the work carried out by those in the research department was studied by Stanier and he took note of the qualifications and abilities of those responsible. Ever since he had arrived on the LMS from Swindon, Stanier had begun to mould the three design teams available to him, at Derby, Crewe and Horwich, into an integrated whole, his predecessor Fowler having left the constitution untouched in the hope that Derby would prove pre-eminent and eclipse the other two. Instead, the old inter-company rivalry had lived on, to the detriment of the locomotive policy, in that the old MR small engine policy survived much too long. Stanier had established his offices at Euston and was busy picking his team now that the restocking programme was under way and he could see the possible members of that team from the efforts of those involved. Ron's work clearly came through as solid and dependable and so he was chosen for transfer to the CME's offices there. Apparently, this transfer was an exchange with a colleague of earlier days, so Ron queried this, but was told firmly that the CME's Department took precedence over all. The posting also meant that he could return to live at home and get involved in the model railway scene again.

Being back at home and based at Euston gave Ron the opportunity to join the Model Railway Club (MRC). He and Jim had been updating and rebuilding much of the existing stock and locomotives. Their efforts resulted in models of a much higher standard than hitherto and some of their efforts were displayed at the MRC annual exhibitions then held at the Central Hall, Westminster.

After a short time of settling in at the CME's offices in Drummond Street he was put into Thomas Hornbuckle's team, where he was to gain much useful experience. Hornbuckle had been proposing the consideration of diesel

An example of Ron's model-making skills. A freelance 0-6-2T, inspired by Beyer, Peacock clockwork mechanism.   *J.M. Jarvis*

The 'Gorselands' outdoor layout.   *J.M. Jarvis*

motive power for many years and sent Ron out on several investigative trips
to assess the experimental use of this type of propulsive medium then taking
place on the LMS. The first assignment was to inspect and report on the
Leyland railcars in service on the railway in the Midlands and North-West.
These vehicles had been on trial since early 1934, and the service Ron assessed
was that running between Spring Vale and Gisburn. They were stabled at
Lower Darwen Shed, where he was welcomed by the shed foreman, Mr
Adams, and taken to inspect car No. 29552, which had been prepared by
removal of all access covers. Later that day, the 18th August, he made several
trips on this example on the branch, and was given the opportunity to drive it
on a couple of runs. These simple 4-wheel railcars were averaging some 1,200-
1,400 miles a week in service with good reliability, with a fuel consumption of
around 14-15 miles per gallon.

A few days later, on the 24th August, he was sent to assess a Sentinel-Cammell
railcar and trailer being tested on the LMS. This was an export design for the
Peruvian Railways, and as it could cope with a trailing load was of particular
interest to the LMS. The assessment run commenced in the Metropolitan-Cammell
yard connected to the main line and terminated at Wolverhampton yard.

One little interesting investigative study to follow the railcar episodes which
came Ron's way was to assess the practicality of what was termed the
Telemotor Control Gear. This interesting project permitted a locomotive to be
driven from the leading coach of a train, thus eliminating a run-round at the end
of a journey, with the engine propelling the train. The train involved for this set
of trials was a seven-car set of Tilbury stock and a 3-cylinder 2-6-4T.

Shortly after this the team under Hornbuckle was given the task of planning the
development of a 3-car diesel train, some prototypes of which were to be built.
The GWR had begun introducing diesel railcars on cross-country and branch
lines and their potential was clearly proven. The LMS plan was based on study of
the German 'Flying Hamburger' units which had been operating a high speed
service between Berlin and Hamburg since 1933. Also, in the UK, studies of
similar units had been made by private industry, the most promising coming
from Beardmore and Co. Study of the Beardmore proposal shows a strong
resemblance between the layout of this and the resulting LMS study but there the
comparison ends. Beardmore's had proposed a 500 horse-power diesel engine
driving an electric generator feeding power to motors on the bogies. The
Hornbuckle design eventually chosen employed six 125 hp diesel engines with
individual hydraulic transmission sets driving six of the eight axles. Hornbuckle's
original proposal for the diesel set was to fit the equipment to three light standard
coaches to be run as a two- or three-coach train. For this unit Leyland Motors were
willing to supply the engines and control equipment free of charge if the trials
proved the experiment unsuccessful. However, this advantageous proposal was
speedily scuppered by Stanier, who was, at that time, very interested in
developing lightweight coach construction methods, which led to a switch to an
all-new unit incorporating this latter technique.

Hornbuckle was the logical choice to lead this study, for he had been
involved in much of the diesel shunter developments then taking place on the
LMS. He had joined the MR in the early days of the century as an Electrical

This 1865 design of 0-4-0T was still in use at Crewe works in 1933 as a works shunter, seen here attached to a cab for dignitaries/senior staff.   *R.G. Jarvis Collection*

Leyland 4-wheeled rail bus of 1934.   *Jarvis Collection*

Engineer, rising to the position of Chief Technical Assistant (Electrical) to the CME during Fowler's incumbency, which position he retained on the accession of Stanier. He had started as an apprentice with Hornsby and Sons, one of the pioneering firms involved in the development of oil engines, so his knowledge of the diesel developments was very sound.

As with the Beardmore design, the LMS set was streamlined, and a model was prepared for testing in a wind-tunnel facility which was being installed in part of Derby works paint shop as Ron departed from the Research Department. This new facility was almost immediately put to use in testing different shapes being considered for the articulated dmu.

The engines eventually selected were of a new type developed especially for rail use by Leyland Motors Limited, producing 125 bhp at 2,200 rpm. Driving was from either of the end cabs, with control of the engines through an electro-pneumatic system. This system had been developed by Dr H.F. Hayworth and his staff at Leyland Motors, derived from successful applications in single and twin-engined railcars. Their purpose had been to achieve a reliable control system for multiple unit operations of diesel torque convertor power units, so that any number of equipments could be installed in a train to provide the power required.

Authorisation to proceed being funded, Ron spent much time up at Derby carriage and wagon works as construction got under way, his collaborator on the production side being George Smithyman. Originally it had been hoped to build two sets, but a change of specification caused an increase in cost per unit and to keep within the funding limits one set only could be produced. The CME, W.A. Stanier, had insisted on increasing the power available in order that high speeds could be attained, as he said at the time, 'Gresley has demonstrated 113 mph (on a scheduled run with the streamlined Pacific No. 2512 *Silver Fox*) on the LNER, so the LMS must do 120!'

The bodies of the dmu were of lightweight construction similar to new electric stock then being developed for the Liverpool-Southport line. The prototype unit was completed in early 1938 and, after initial trials in the vicinity of Derby started going further afield. On 25th February two trial runs to Buxton were made during which speeds of up to 67 mph were attained. The following day more runs to Buxton achieved 74 mph. A gradient of 1 in 132 was climbed at a steady 70 mph on another run to Cheadle Heath. By 2nd March matters were sufficient to warrant a main line run to Gloucester and back. The log of this run still exists and appears here as *Table One*. On the return trip the unit was stopped at Bromsgrove in order to try it out from a standing start up the Lickey Bank. A speed of 39 mph was achieved up this incline, leaving the thoughtfully provided banker way behind from the start.

Following analysis of the performance on trial, the unit was moved to Wolverton to work on the Oxford-Cambridge cross-country route for extended trials. Servicing and any maintenance was to be carried out at the Wolverton carriage works near Bletchley on that route. Ron was one of two members of the Euston team delegated to supervise the performance, servicing and running repairs. His colleague taking alternate turns with him was E.R.M. Montague. As, over the next few weeks, their duties required temporary accommodation near Wolverton, they found some digs in Bletchley, the landlady remarking one day,

The 3-car dmu takes shape at Derby carriage and wagon works, June 1937. *Jarvis Collection*

The dmu at Gloucester awaits the return journey to Derby. Compound No. 1073 on left.
R.G. Jarvis Collection

The 3-car diesel on trial passes through Blunham station.   *R.G. Jarvis Collection*

Ron Jarvis stands in front of the 3-car diesel train.   *Jarvis Collection*

During the dmu trials between Oxford and Cambridge the Stirling 'Single' No. 1 appeared at Cambridge on a Special. Ron just happened to be there with his camera.

R.G. Jarvis Collection

Table One

3-Car Diesel Unit Test to Gloucester, 2nd March, 1938

		Schedule	Actual	
Derby Carriage Works	dep.		8.02	am
London Road Junction	arr.		8.07	
	dep.	8.12	8.11	
L&NW Junction	pass	8.16	8.15	
Burton	pass	8.30	8.28	
Wichnor Jn	pass	8.37	8.35	
Tamworth	pass	8.46	8.44	
Kingsbury Station Jn	pass	8.55	8.51	
Water Orton Station Jn	pass	9.00	8.58	
Saltley	pass	9.07	9.07	
Camp Hill	pass	9.13	9.14	
Kings Norton	pass	9.19	9.21	
Blackwell	pass	9.27	9.29	
Bromsgrove	pass	9.33	9.35	
Dunhampstead	pass	9.40	9.42	
Ashchurch	pass	9.55	9.59	(signals)
Cheltenham	pass	10.02	10.08	
Gloucester	arr.	10.10	10.14	

The severe signal check at Ashchurch upset what was a creditable attempt to keep to the schedule, which was set for an express passenger train.

		Schedule	Actual	
Gloucester	dep.	11.18	11.15	am
Cheltenham	pass	11.28	11.26	
Ashchurch	pass	11.36	11.33	
Dunhampstead	pass	11.52	11.50	
Bromsgrove	arr.	11.59	11.58	
	dep.		11.59	
Blackwell	pass	12.06	12.03	pm
Barnt Green	arr.		12.06	
	dep.		12.09	
Kings Norton	pass	12.15	12.15	
Camp Hill	pass	12.25	12.21	
Saltley	pass	12.35	12.27	
Water Orton	pass	12.44	12.34	
Kingsbury Station Jn	pass	12.48	12.39	
Tamworth	pass	12.54	12.45	
Wichnor Jn	pass	1.03	12.53	
Burton	pass	1.10	1.05	
L&NW Jn	pass	1.24	1.21	(signals)
London Road Jn	arr.	1.28	1.23	
	dep.	1.32		
Derby Carriage Works	arr.	1.37		

A much better run back to Derby, with time being gained everywhere and a 10 minute gain on schedule until checked by signals outside Derby.

The stop at Bromsgrove was to test the train from a standing start up the Lickey Bank, the banker provided being left behind from the 'right away'.

'You are engineers, aren't you? I can smell you!' No doubt that day they had been at the works in a hands-on capacity and diesel oil had got onto their clothing.

Once the diesel unit had been run in, the management of the LMS arrived to inspect it, being shown over by Ron. He recalled this event in a letter thus:

> I recall being present on the 3-car train when it was inspected by various chief officers, including W.A.S. and E.J.H. Lemon, then Vice-President. Some point was raised when W.A.S. was a little distance from the others, and Lemon whistled him up and called, 'Stanier, come 'ere'. He went like a lamb. I couldn't help remarking to one of the smaller fry with me there: 'How would you like to be able to whistle up the CME like that?'

The trials went quite smoothly, but there were some minor incidents. The first of note being when at maximum speed a partridge flew into the cab window, burst through, hit the driver in the face and finished very dead on his lap. Fortunately, the driver escaped serious injury, only suffering a couple of black eyes. The partridge was not wasted, as the driver took it home for his next Sunday lunch! On another run the train breasted a minor summit only to find, a short distance ahead, a tractor and trailer stalled on an occupation crossing. The tractor driver had the presence of mind to release the coupling pin between the vehicles, whereupon the tractor surged forward and the trailer rolled back. The gap produced was just sufficient for the train to shoot through unharmed!

On many of these test runs Ron drove the unit and started training the drivers who would be taking the train on its service trials. He reported to both Hornbuckle and Stanier during these trials and, having been suitably impressed by the support he had got from Wolverton, suggested to Stanier that a token of thanks might be in order. He himself wrote: 'When the 3-car train had some troubles in 1938 and I had to take it to Wolverton for modifications, the Works Manager, Merrett, and all his team, indeed everyone concerned, really put themselves out to do what was required in double quick time. Afterwards I suggested to W.A.S. that a letter should be written to Merrett, thanking him and his staff for the good work they had done. His reply was, "No, I am not going to write them a letter - you can write them one if you like - aren't they paid to do a good job?"' This rather dismayed Ron, who had a strong sense of fair play and thought good support merited some appreciation.

Engine failure, not a rare occurrence with prototype engines, was fully catered for by each unit having a freewheel capability in that event. However, the result of only having one dmu in service caused some operating limitations when it was out of service for maintenance, the schedule having been speeded up by the excellent accelerative capability and 75 mph top speed of the train. The reversion to steam operation on such a fast service caused some problems for the locomotives crews in their endeavour to meet the schedule, despite the short train length, two or three coaches, of this service. On one such occasion, the locomotive failed completely out in the Bedfordshire countryside. The only ready replacement was an ex-LNWR 'G2' 0-8-0 on some local brickyard traffic duties. This took over the train and, to all accounts, made a creditable effort to minimise further time loss. This must have been quite some sight!

The success of the dmu led to its being put into regular service on 12th September on the Oxford-Cambridge line. By the end of 1938 some 36,366 miles had been run out of 47,124 scheduled. This was followed, in 1939, by turns out of St Pancras on commuter runs and a high-speed service to Nottingham. Unfortunately, the onset of World War II altered priorities in the railway sphere and investment for further dmus was not forthcoming. However, by then, some 90,000 miles had been run with a nearly 80 per cent availability of the single unit. Much interest had been raised, and Hornbuckle and H.F. Haworth of Leyland Motors wrote a paper on the development for presentation to the Institution of Locomotive Engineers, this being given in 1939. Ron had to deal with the reading of this and the ensuing discussion, one author being absent from the proceedings and the other suffering from a sore throat.

By this time the approach of war had resulted in reorganisations, with the majority of the LMS Headquarters staff being moved to Watford and the CME's office being centred on Derby. There was much to be done in setting up production of wartime needs and only 21 new locomotives (one 2-6-4T and 20 '4F' class 0-6-0s) appeared from Derby in 1939. It was really a holding operation so far as the LDO and Research Department were concerned. Ron's time and the way in which he had dealt with his duties on Stanier's team had ensured that he would shortly be entrusted with something of substance to cover.

The dmu was withdrawn from service shortly after the outbreak of the war and never ran again as a train. Hornbuckle, omitted from the Derby move, left the LMS for a top job with the Woolwich Arsenal in the North-East. He corresponded with Ron for many years and his letters clearly point to a very high regard of his assistant's abilities. Perhaps a good opinion emanating from Ron of Hornbuckle is graphically illustrated in one of his letters of 1941, 'Tommy has a philosophy of life that is an inspiration and tonic and it was indeed a privilege to work for him'.

The dmu was stored throughout the war and lay neglected until 1949, when it was cannibalised to provide chassis and power units for a service train to be used for installation and maintenance of overhead suspension units on electrified lines. So ended a pioneering dmu exercise.

One important event had happened whilst all the dmu work was taking place, this being that Ron had met the girl who was to become his wife. He first met May Baldock at a Tennis Club dance in Harpenden that all the Jarvis family attended in early 1937. The club, Elliswick Tennis Club, had been founded by their father in the 1920s as, being a builder, he was technically a tradesman and not eligible for membership of the established tennis club then. May had known Geoffrey and his sister Heather for some time and had not realised that Ron and Jim were around - until that dance! Ron soon joined the club and a friendship began. May worked as a Secretary at the Railway Clearing House (RCH) in Eversholt Street, next to Euston station. They discovered that they travelled up to St Pancras on the 8.10 non-stop from Harpenden. May was frequently a last minute joiner and Ron would hold the door open for her as she ran for the train. They had much in common and the friendship blossomed, to be interrupted by the onset of the war when the RCH was evacuated to Amersham and Ron returned to Derby. Another feature of Ron's and May's backgounds was that May's father had been a railwayman with the Great Northern Railway and then LNER, retiring in 1934, and her sister Lily also worked at the RCH.

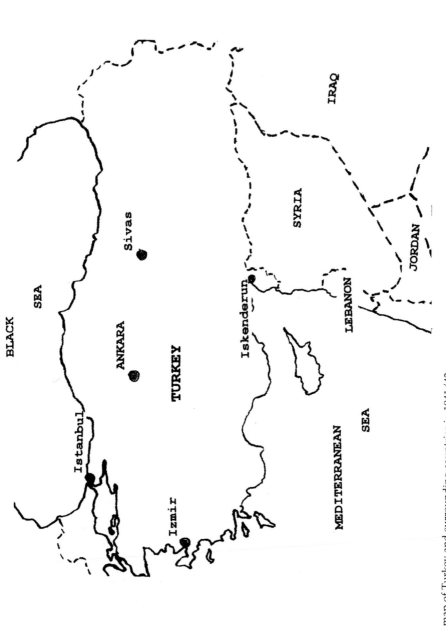

A map of Turkey and surrounding countries in 1941/42

Chapter Three

The War Years - A Voyage to Turkey

With the lay-up of the dmu, Ron returned permanently to the CME's Department to tidy up the programme results, which kept him occupied in odd moments between other railway business. Then he was assigned to the staff of George Ivatt, who had been released from his earlier position of Chief Assistant to Stanier to oversee tank design and production contracted out by the War Department. The tank involved was the 'Covenanter' and he spent some time on the production side of things. With the war changing priorities at work, Ron, after Dunkirk, joined the Derby Home Guard in order to help him feel that, even in his reserved occupation, he could do something to prepare for the anticipated invasion.

The first major assignment for him in the early war years was brought about by the need to supply some '8F' class 2-8-0s to Turkey. This resulted from an outstanding order from the Turkish State Railways for freight locomotives which was current as war broke out. This order was for a specific export 2-10-0 type of, ironically, a German design, placed with the North British Locomotive Company. Due to the reorganisation in the railways and private builders' factories this particular order could no longer be fulfilled in the time expected. Much effort was being made to keep Turkey aligned with the UK, in that technical assistance to the Turkish Government in many fields was under way. The Air Force of that state had recently been supplied with British aircraft and members of the RAF were there advising on the development of airfields in Turkey. Also, plans were afoot to 'infiltrate' 10 to 15 RAF squadrons into Turkey to counter anticipated German penetration of nearby Bulgaria with its strategic oil-fields. The locomotive order was a key part of the many-faceted aid programme and the successful completion of this would help further cement Anglo-Turkish relations so carefully nurtured over the pre-war and early war years.

Diplomatic moves were made in high places resulting in the Stanier '8F' class being substituted for the 2-10-0. This made sense, as the War Department had placed substantial orders for the '8F' which was to be used in overseas service. Production had commenced at the North British and Beyer, Peacock works in addition to further batches appearing from Crewe, and eventually Swindon, Horwich, Doncaster, Darlington, Eastleigh, Ashford and Brighton, so a quick fulfilment of the Turkish requirement could be made with minimum disruption to production schedules. The transaction was carried out by the United Kingdom Commercial Corporation (UKCC), a hand-maiden of the British Government, and the 'go-between' for many important commercial transactions in the Middle East in those days. The only concession made in this order was to provide the locomotive with right-hand drive and air brakes to conform with Turkish standards.

It was planned to ship out the locomotives in a partially broken down condition, necessitating reassembly in Turkey. The LMS were to supply key personnel to oversee this reassembly. Some urgency was afoot, as it was feared that the Germans might make moves to grab this order, their standard 2-10-0 being of similar specification to that of the original requirement and was in mass production. Such a matter could not be contemplated, as it would give Germany a key to the access of the Near and Middle East. Turkey was biased towards the UK and the continued pressure on their Government eventually ensured that the order, as amended, stayed in place.

In late 1940 Ron was told that he had been chosen to oversee the supply and assembly programme. He would have one assistant, a Fred Soden, a foreman from Crewe works, who would be there to supervise and instruct on the fitting tasks of the reassembly. Soden had accompanied the 'Coronation' Pacific to the USA in 1939, as master mechanic, and so journeys overseas were not new to him. He was to prove an extremely capable assistant.

May was now an important part of his life, the friendship having been drawn closer by their enforced parting over the early months of the war. When the Turkish trip was intimated, he realised that a time apart was imminent and, having decided that this was definitely the lady for him, popped the obvious question. To his delight, May accepted his proposal and they began to plan for a wedding when he returned from his foreign trip.

Before setting off from Paddington to Swansea, where he was to join the ship taking him and Soden to Turkey, Ron and May, together with Fred Soden, passed a pleasant evening at the Strand Palace Hotel at a farewell dinner at which there was dancing. Fred loved dancing and was delighted when May asked him for a turn on the floor. He was to enthuse about this over the months that followed. The engagement was not on the agenda, as Ron and May had decided to keep this within their respective families in the meantime.

In the spring of 1941, Ron and his assistant set sail from Swansea for Turkey via the Cape of Good Hope on the Swedish twin-screw motor ship *Shantung* of 6,500 tons. This vessel was owned and operated by the Swedish East-Asiatic Line of Gothenburg. In addition to Ron and Fred there were seven other passengers. The crew were all Swedish and the captain was accompanied by his dog, an Alsatian bitch relishing in the name of 'Yippie'. Ron and Fred shared a well-fitted and comfortable cabin.

Once at sea the reality of war appeared in the form of several Dorniers dropping magnetic mines around them on the first night. There was fierce defence from the nearby escorts' anti-aircraft guns aided by searchlights and one of the bombers came down in the sea. They waited for the mines to be swept and then sailed, in convoy, up the Irish Sea and out into the Atlantic. Once *en route* there was much spare time and Ron applied himself to studying Turkish, using text-books he had bought in London. A matter which caused some discomfort was the order for all on board to wear their clothes 24 hours a day, so that, if torpedoed, they would be ready to abandon ship in the minimum of time. This was especially important as they crossed the cold waters of the North Atlantic.

Their escorts consisted of five destroyers, one corvette and an armed trawler. As they neared Iceland the convoy was scattered, as news that the *Scharnhorst* battleship and heavy cruiser *Gneisenau* were heading into the North Atlantic had been radioed to the Navy escorts. Each ship was to look after itself. The next they heard of them was of their arrival in Brest, after the Royal Navy had launched a huge search operation for the raiders. As Ron himself noted much later, 'A case of ships that pass in the night'.

There was not much to do when at sea, so Ron busied himself in investigating the ship. One day he caught a rat, of which there were quite a few on board, and threw it overboard. Shortly after this he was talking to the captain and told of his dealing with the stowaway, and was told that sailor's folklore marked that as an unlucky omen. Tragically, the *Shantung* was sunk on its next voyage. When Ron died his widow found that he had been carrying in his wallet, since that time, a newspaper cutting about the loss of the ship.

Their first port of call was Freetown, followed by Cape Town, which was reached at Easter. This visit was quite lengthy, for their ship, having entered the Southern Hemisphere needed de-Gaussing again to counter the reversed polarity of the Earth's magnetic field. Ron and Fred were greatly relieved to be able to spend a few days ashore and left the ship for the Carlton Hotel. There was no rationing in South Africa and they took advantage of the local restaurant's selections of dishes. A trip up Table Mountain was somewhat spoilt by the low cloud hanging over it, and several invitations to visit local homes came flooding in from families with relatives in the United Kingdom. 'This has been a very pleasant surprise here and quite a nice little holiday in itself', Ron wrote to May in a letter posted from Cape Town.

Their next stop was Aden, followed by a hot passage up the Red Sea to Suez. This last part of their voyage was now much safer with the Italians having been defeated and cleared out of East Africa just a few weeks earlier.

As they had done during the voyage through the tropics to South Africa, the crew of the *Shantung* rigged up the temporary canvas swimming pool on deck as the vessel sailed north through the Indian Ocean towards Aden. It was hot on board in those regions and Ron took several daily dips in the welcome coolness of the pool as they voyaged on.

By 3rd May they were well up the Red Sea *en route* to Suez. Land could not be far off now, for there were vultures perched in the rigging! Two nights later, before they made landfall, there was a farewell dinner for crew and passengers. A great spread was prepared and plenty of alcoholic beverages accompanied each course for the many and varied toasts. Ron described the result of this in one of his letters to May, 'Most of us were a bit tight!'

It was during this voyage that the German offensive on the Balkans began, a feature which was to affect the war in the vicinity of Turkey but, with the locomotives being prepared for shipping and the supervisory team *en route*, matters were set for completion of a daunting task.

As the Suez Canal had been mined, the voyage terminated at Suez with Ron and his companion disembarking. Bidding farewell to the crew, they proceeded to Cairo by train to find out how the rest of the journey to Turkey was to be accomplished. The weather was extremely hot, 123°F in the shade, as they settled into the National Hotel in the noisy bustle of the Egyptian capital. After reporting their presence to the UKCC office a few hours were spent in taking a trip to the pyramids and viewing the small, well-kept Cairo Zoo.

Although Ron had a camera with him in Turkey no known pictures were taken due to current wartime restrictions. This was sent to him by Captain Alexander of the tugboat *Amiral Lacaze* and depicts ships at anchor in the bay off Iskenderun.

R.G. Jarvis Collection

After a couple of days wait they continued to Alexandria where they eventually boarded a freighter bound for the port of Iskenderun in South East Turkey. The Germans were now at the Western border of Turkey, Greece had fallen and the British forces were being driven out of Crete. In nearby Iraq, Rashid Ali was creating immense trouble and trying to overthrow the British presence in that country. Also, Vichy France had opened its airfields in Syria and the Lebanon to the Luftwaffe, which threatened sea communications between Egypt and Turkey, so events were not all going the Allies way in that part of the world. At this time Russia still had in place a treaty of friendship with Germany. Turkey appeared to be surrounded.

Landing at Iskenderun, a first glance at the port facilities showed that there was much to be done shortly to make it suitable for the landing of large, heavy crates. Ron and his assistant then travelled by rail to Istanbul to visit the offices of the UKCC and report their arrival. To both of them the presence of the enemy there made it a difficult place to be, and no sightseeing was undertaken. A few days cooling their heels in Istanbul passed before orders to go to Ankara arrived.

By 21st June they were in Ankara at the Belviic Palace Hotel. The capital of Turkey was being thoroughly modernised and the food was tolerably good. Wide streets and new office blocks and buildings had replaced the older buildings and the lack of a blackout made the nights vibrant and alive. Much of their time was spent at the British Embassy, where the UKCC staff proved most helpful in getting matters under way. Ron made arrangements for mail to be routed through the diplomatic bag system, for he was sure that Stanier, Ivatt and Fairburn would need to be kept in touch with developments as events unfolded.

Initially it was decided that Ron and Fred should be based at Iskenderun. There was a British Consulate there and this port was to be used for the shipping in of the locomotives and wagons. After a week in Ankara they caught the 'Taurus Express' for the first part of their 24 hour journey to Eastern Turkey.

With the war situation as it stood now, the only Turkish port easily accessible for the import of the locomotives and wagons was in fact that at Iskenderun. This had previously been known as Alexandretta and had been a French colony. To the north of that port lay the Taurus mountains and to the south-east the Anti-Taurus ranges rose. A short distance to the south lay the biblical town of Antioch. The early summer weather was hot and humid.

After enduring a few days in the blistering heat of Iskenderun, Ron found the Tuirizm Hotel at Nerquizlik, 1,500 feet up in the mountains behind the coast. This was cooler and, once the bed-bugs had been dealt with, tolerably comfortable. It also had a fine view of the Bay of Iskenderun some 12 miles away, and a local bus service of erratic timing served to get them to and from the port.

Unfortunately, the hotel proved to be a short-lived episode and they had to move back to the coast because of the unreliability of the bus. Ron based himself in the UKCC office in the Consulate which stood in the hills just behind Iskenderun. However, the stay there was at last made tolerable in the heat of the summer by being recommended to accommodation with a Mme Psychopolous

Plan of Port of Iskenderun as drawn up by Ron to assist the authorities in preparing the necessary changes.

R.G. Jarvis Collection

and her sister, which, as Ron wrote, '. . . was a very nice house where we were very comfortable for nearly two months. These are very good digs if you can get in'.

Returning to Iskerendun, Ron's first task was to ensure that the required alterations and improvements to the port itself were satisfactory for the offloading of the crates, many weighing 25 tons, containing the locomotives and wagons parts to be reassembled. To ensure that the large crates could be transported away easily, much extra standard gauge track was being laid around the docks, to plans prepared by Ron, and which already had its own metre gauge system. Some cranes needed urgent repairs. Also, to ensure that all in the port was in the best order possible, Ron undertook a survey of the metre gauge railway around the docks concentrating on the condition of the locomotives. There were three stored there, all 0-4-0 well tanks built by Borsig in 1911. Nos. 1 and 8 were in repairable condition, but the third, No. 2, had been cannibalised and was only worth scrapping. Sufficient spares were available for the repairs and this information was transmitted to the authorities. As the ships bringing the locomotives had to anchor out in the bay and tranship their loads onto lighters, tugs were needed, one of which, the *Amiral Lacaze*, required urgent repairs after running agound at Mitylene. Ron, in his unofficial capacity of Consulting Engineer, assessed the damage and wrote a report for the UKCC so that they could pass this through to the appropriate Turkish authority.

Unfortunately, the first consignment of locomotives, due in early summer, had been sunk and four '8Fs' lie somewhere on the ocean bottom. The follow-up batches were gradually being dispatched, but were somewhat swallowed up in the vast amount of supplies then being shipped to the Middle East. A delay in matters seemed inevitable. Meantime, the war had taken a dramatic turn with the German invasion of Russia. It looked as though Turkey would soon be totally surrounded and cut off but, after the Iraqi menace of Rashid Ali had been overthrown near Habbaniya, the Allied forces in Palestine and Iraq invaded Syria and soon had the Vichy French defeated. The way was now open for unhindered shipping runs from Egypt to Turkey. However, the German Afrika Korps was threatening Egypt and temporarily held on the border with Libya. So all efforts were being channelled towards the speedy build-up of supplies and equipment to stem this relentless onslaught. It was not surprising that the sorely needed locomotives and wagons were dumped at Alexandria and Suez amongst the tons of other supplies. The needs of the armed forces came first.

In desperation Ron dispatched Fred Soden to the Canal Zone with the task of finding and identifying the delayed crates due for forwarding to Iskerendun, and arranging their delivery.

Meantime, there was a dramatic indication of the turnabout in Syria, by the arrival in Iskenderun Bay of a varied collection of French warships surrendering to neutral Turkey. All in that part of Turkey were greatly relieved at the occupation of Syria, for now the forces across the border were friendly and the threat of the Luftwaffe removed. Ron mentioned in one of his letters the drone of aircraft one night at about the time the British invasion of Syria took place. This probably was the Luftwaffe withdrawing to the relative safety of Greece.

As all the above took place, Ron's brother, Geoffrey, was married. Ron was sorry to miss this great family gathering but cabled his congratulations to the happy couple. His letters home contained much detail about the happenings whilst they waited for delivery of the locomotives. 'I sometimes make myself useful to them (the various Turkish Authorities/Consulate staff, etc.) repairing this and that - motor cars, motor boats, duplicators, and refrigerators to say nothing of the bigger stuff like locos, cranes and diesel tugs!'

So, as he waited patiently for events to unfold, his time and engineering expertise was not being wasted, although the main task of overseeing erection of the locomotives and wagons could still not begin. Soden was still in Egypt chasing up and locating the crates languishing at Alexandria amongst the huge stockpile of military equipment flooding in.

Although Ron took no pictures of the Sivas-built '8Fs', in later years his brother Jim did. Here is one, Turkish Railways No. 45170, caught at Samsun in 1983, some 42 years after construction!   *J.M. Jarvis*

Chapter Four

Assembling Locomotives in Wartime Turkey

With Fred Soden away in Egypt and it being obvious that some delay in shipping the locomotives and wagons was inevitable, Ron was requested by the UKCC to organise the British Pavilion at the Izmir Trade Fair. He flew to Ankara and travelled from there to Izmir by train, establishing himself at the Izmir Palace Hotel. This assignment was quite a novel challenge. The pavilion was to have backdrop scenes, some of which depicted the Suez Canal. Ron cast around locally and found some Armenian artists who were engaged to paint the backdrop. They were competent enough for much of the work but needed some guidance on the depiction of large ships in the canal scenes. Ron sketched their outline on the canvas enabling the artists to make credible pictures. The pavilion was one of a group of three, the centre one representing Turkey and the ones on either side being the British and the German displays. At the opening ceremony Ron had the privilege of escorting the President of Turkey, Ismet Inonii, around his display. The German pavilion was magnificent, no expense had been spared but, according to Ron, the Turks hated it because of its generally cold artistic splendour.

Being a neutral country, Turkey was host to various nationalities, and the Germans were there in some numbers. One evening Ron was dining at a fashionable restaurant in Izmir which was used by many of the foreign dignitaries. A few tables away sat Herr von Papen, the German Ambassador, entertaining some colleagues, whilst in the background an orchestra, comprised of local musicians, played. Nearby sat some RAF officers in civilian garb who clearly wished to try out von Papen's sense of humour. They managed to bribe the players to strike up in his honour, 'We can't give you anything but love, Baby!' There is no record of the response, probably it was received in stony silence.

Ron's ability to speak and write French fluently proved very useful in Turkey in corresponding with many of the officials who spoke that language. Letters still exist showing his command of it.

With the end of the Trade Fair, 8th September found him *en route* for Iskenderun and stopping off at Ankara to call in at the British Embassy for an update. Matters in Egypt were at last moving. Soden had located some of the crates containing wagon parts and was arranging shipment. Ron returned to Iskenderun to check on the status of the docks improvements and awaited more news from Alexandria. Soden had sent back not very encouraging news, this being that he had found most of the crates buried under mountains of military supplies. Many of the crates had been badly damaged in transit and it looked as though some of the components were damaged and corroding. It seemed that considerable confusion reigned at Alexandria and the forwarding was likely to be delayed. However, efforts were being made to arrange the shipping of the first locomotives as soon as possible. The greatest problem in their carriage was to find ships with deck cranes having a 25 ton capacity to cope with the crates

The UKCC stand at the 1941 Izmir Trade Fair as designed and erected under Ron Jarvis.

R.G. Jarvis Collection

Part of the exhibits on the UKCC stand. The locomotives in the picture appear to be based on the Stanier 'Black Five'. *Inset:* The Izmir Trade Fair brochure. *(Both) R.G. Jarvis Collection*

containing the boilers and frames of the '8Fs'. Using Iskenderun, involved anchoring out in the bay and off-loading the cargoes into lighters for transhipment ashore.

Assembly of the locomotives and wagons was to take place at the Turkish State Railways plant at Sivas in the Anatolian Highlands. It was at a height of some 4,500 feet. This plant had only been built two years ago, by the Germans, and thus all the equipment installed was of the best quality. Ron wrote home to Riddles: 'The Sivas works is a fine layout, well equipped with most things, and well adapted for repairs of locos, wagons and carriages. It is two years old and therefore the staff are not all well experienced, but as Turkish enterprises go, this is an exceptionally efficient undertaking, and in that respect we are lucky'.

By the end of September Ron had left Iskenderun and relocated to Sivas, travelling on the 'Taurus Express' as far as Kayserii where he changed for a through train for Eastern Turkey which called at Sivas. The best hotel in Sivas was the Cumhuriyet which was a great come-down from the earlier establishments at Ankara, Izmir and Iskenderun. It was infested with bugs, dirty and the food was atrocious. But it was the best hotel in the town, so Ron stoically settled down, waging war on the bugs and making the best of a bad job. There was no time to search around for something better as the first crates containing wagon parts had arrived. On 4th October the first wagon was completed and the production line set up for the 600 plus to roll out of Sivas works over the following months.

Ron was well received by the management of the works, who proved friendly and co-operative now that matters were underway at last. To assist in his getting to know them better a series of social activities were arranged, beginning with a dinner at the Assistant Works Manager's house. On 9th October the Turkish Minister of Communication paid an official visit to the works and asked specifically to meet Ron. The production of wagons was now at two a day. The next day the Assistant CME of the Turkish State railways, Hakki Bey, arrived in his service carriage from Ankara on a liaison visit. The carriage was fitted out for dining and Ron, together with the management of the works, dined there that evening.

The town of Sivas itself was another matter altogether, as Ron wrote:

Sivas is a real old-fashioned place quite like you see in films of mediaeval England. The streets are roughly paved, and the houses, built of timber and white-washed mud bricks, have a tumbledown appearance. Until about ten years ago, when the railway was opened to Sivas, the town had little connection to the outside world.

So in such a basic environment it seemed very unusual to find a modern railway works.

On 20th October, Fred Soden arrived back to join Ron. His time in Egypt had located much of the missing stock and arrangements were made with the UKCC to see to the shipping. Some locomotives were now in transit. The wagon production rate had risen to four a day. The first locomotive parts arrived shortly after Fred, and erection began. Ron's command of Turkish, although enough for day-to-day conversation, was not adequate enough for shop-floor instructions and he had great difficulty in impressing on the workers the need to follow set procedures for the assembly of the '8Fs'. Matters were not helped by the obvious fact that North British had never assembled them completely during production, so delays occurred as the inexperienced workers struggled to fit some of the parts. Despite this, the first complete '8F' rolled out in December 1941.

Once installed in Sivas, and with time to look around, Ron and Fred rented a house:

> Or perhaps it should be called a flat. The hotels in Sivas (and Turkey generally) are cold (or if centrally heated, uncomfortably hot), they are infested with that delightful little fellow, the bed bug, and the service is non-existent. We are comfortable in our little house, except that the lavatory is on the balcony outside, and believe us it is a cold job!

That year the winter had arrived early and the first snows were falling in the mountains around them.

Their presence in Sivas was unique, as it transpired they were the first Englishmen to live in that town, but the locals treated them very kindly and eased their integration into what seemed a totally alien way of life. Whilst in Summer it could be unbearably hot, Winter temperatures sometimes plunged to minus 30 degrees centigrade, and they had been sent out with tropical kit!

Some of the language difficulties were overcome by the presence of a Sivas carriage and wagon foreman, Sadettin Bey, who spoke good English and had spent some time at Derby and Crewe works before the war. On administrative matters, the C. & W. Manager, Nuri Bey, was a good and helpful friend to both Ron and Fred Soden.

On his initial travels around Turkey, Ron had encountered a fair cross-section of the Turkish railway sphere and described this in a letter to Fairburn in September 1941:

> Except for the British influence of the old Ottoman Railway Company in the Izmir district, the railways here are predominantly German, and that means complicated engines and heavy carriages (45 tons apiece). The Ottoman Railway, known as the Aidin, is a refreshing change, for here you see pretty little English types - 0-6-0, 0-6-2T, 2-4-0, and 0-4-0ST etc., as well as large 0-8-0, 2-8-2, and 0-8-2T built by R. Stephenson. The carriages are only 27 tons, and are of similar design to the B.A.P. I had great pleasure the other day seeing a Dean 0-6-0 still with GWR built Swindon on its plate. All these English engines are held in great affection by the men.

November saw the more locomotives arriving and five were completed before Christmas. Each locomotive was shipped in 23 cases, being made up of one chassis complete with cylinders, eight separate pairs of wheels, one boiler, one tender chassis, one tender tank and 11 other boxes in which all the small parts were packed. It took approximately 10 or 11 days to erect each locomotive after any remedial work caused by damage or corrosion had been undertaken. In the works, Ron found Fred Soden an excellent help on the shop floor, 'A real good loco man and had plenty of common sense' was a typical comment.

As soon as practicable after initial trials, the first '8F' was taken to Ankara for demonstration to the authorities. It was there three days, one of which was Ron's birthday, which was celebrated by a visit to a good restaurant for dinner with Fred and Hakki Bey. As was usual, this restaurant was well patronised by the Germans and the resident band took little persuading to strike up *There'll always be an England.*

In addition to the five locomotives assembled some 216 wagons were completed by 7th December. Initial trials of the reassembled engines quickly presented a problem, that of poor steaming, with Ron reporting in a letter to Stanier:

Our first troubles with the engines arose from the poor coal, which is practically all slack, of low calorific value, and the engines behaved most unsatisfactorily. I have carried out a large number of tests, and found to my disappointment that no simple expedient such as a slight reduction of the blast-pipe orifice did the trick. So I designed a new blast-pipe cap, basing my modifications on those which cured the 5X ('Jubilee' 4-6-0 of the LMS) engines viz:- a lowering of about 4 in. and a reduction in diameter of ⅜ in. We have fitted a simple casting, and have also eliminated the jumper.

However, events saw this careful approach cast to the winds, as:

So we were endeavouring to find just the right blastpipe diameter, when we were called to Ankara to discuss the matter with the Chef de Traction. On our return, we found that the Sivas people had fitted an engine with a 126 mm blast-pipe and a permanent 'Jimmy' of 12 mm width. The Works Manager had already made a trip with this, and reported very favourably. We proceeded to test the engine with 450 tons over the mountain line to Etinkaya, with long sections of 15/1000 combined with sharp curves. The tests were completely satisfactory, and the engine maintained full pressure, and water level, keeping up about 10 to 12 mph in 45 to 50 per cent cut-off. I am inclined to think that for this kind of work the cylinders might be a little larger so as to enable more expansion to be employed. Anyway everyone was so satisfied with the performance, that the railway administration engineers decided there and then to adopt the 'Jimmy', and so your engines are now fitted with this rather fearsome device!

It was then discovered that this crude, but effective, method was virtually standard on most locomotives in Turkey, the German standard Reichsbahn types included and Ron concluded: 'There is now no complaint of steaming from the Turkish people. So my feeling is that the best political outlook is to be satisfied too'.

The steaming problems largely dealt with, Ron turned his mind to designing a drop grate to assist in clearing the clinker which tended to accumulate from the poor quality fuel. He had, by now, virtually given up trying to impress on the running sheds' staff on the need to care for the oiling round on a regular basis. So it was not surprising when one of the first batch limped in with a hot box shortly after entering traffic.

Once the workforce had gained experience on the erection of the '8Fs', the production rate was governed by the speed of delivery of the components which was still slow. Additionally six of the sets of parts had spent no less than six months in storage at Alexandria, resulting in very bad corrosion, especially to the motion parts. Complete repainting was undertaken on many frames plus straightening and repairing of damaged components.

December was, in one respect, a good month, in that 13 more locomotives had arrived at Iskenderun. However, the weather, in the form of deep snow up in the mountains closing the railway, had other plans concerning the delivery.

TELEPHONE:
EUSTON 1234.

Chairman's Room.
Euston Station, London, N.W.1

27th February, 1942

Dear Mr. Jarvis,

I was gratified to receive the enclosed letter
from the Ministry of Supply, and the Board yesterday
expressed their pleasure that your work in Turkey had
been so fully appreciated by both the Foreign Office
and the Ministry of Supply.

I am very glad you so fully upheld the L.M.S.
traditions in this matter.

Yours sincerely,

T. Royden

R. G. Jarvis, Esq.,
Cer Atelyesi, SIVAS,
TURKEY.
(C/o. U.K.C.C. Plantation House,
Fenchurch Street,
LONDON.)

The covering letter sent by the Chairman of the LMS to Ron thanking him for the work carried
out in Turkey.
Jarvis Collection

Christmas 1941 was work as usual. However, Ron and Fred were presented with a Christmas tree by Nuri Bey, the Assistant Works Manager. Decorations in the form of ornaments and tinsel were loaned by Mme Nuri Bey. On Boxing night they hosted a party at their flat with Nuri Bey, four charge-hands/foremen from the works and a Mr Lucas of the UKCC as guests.

Ron passed much of his time designing the drop grate and issuing the drawings for the works to begin manufacturing the parts.

By the middle of February nine '8Fs' were completed and more crates were arriving from Iskenderun. There were now 16 locomotives in Turkey ranging from complete to a set of parts. The end was in sight and by the end of March Ron felt able to go to Ankara and make tentative arrangements for returning home. On his return from that trip locomotives Nos. 15 and 16 were under erection. There was, however, no sign of Nos. 17 and 18.

Both Ron and Fred Soden were bolstered by a personal letter from the LMS Chairman, Sir Thomas Royden, who sent a copy of a communication from the Ministry of Supply thanking the LMS for its co-operation in the supply of personnel to oversee the erection of the locomotives and wagons in Turkey.

In early February, one of the new '8Fs' suffered a failure which necessitated it being taken out of service. The left-hand cylinder was severely damaged whilst the engine was running fast on a down grade with steam shut off. Examination of the offending part showed that the piston, front cylinder cover and cylinder casting were broken, the piston rod was bent and scored and the back cylinder cover bruised at the gland. The extreme weather conditions in winter often led to engines out of service having frozen cylinder drain cocks, which if not cleared can cause some friction in the cylinder on starting. It was thought that this may have cracked the cast-iron piston. Later when running at high speed without any cushioning (i.e. a fully closed regulator), the piston collapsed, and the broken parts caused the remainder of the damage before the engine could be brought to a halt. Ron wrote a comprehensive report on this failure and organised the fitting of a spare cylinder and the machining of a new piston and piston rod. The locomotive was back in service before the end of the month.

In Sivas there was no local restaurant with a radio tuned to the BBC English language broadcasts, so Ron and his companion invested in a brand-new Marconi seven-valve set. Thanks to the local electrical arrangements and a very antique telegraph installation in the nearby post office, the interference was appalling, especially in the daytime. Following a move to other accommodation elsewhere in the town, the reception improved considerably. They listened to the 7.00 am Forces news and adjoining programmes. Daytime reception was very poor until about 5.00 pm and then improved to near perfect in the evenings. Their British presence was advertised, as Ron wrote:

With our set we could get at least three times the volume we normally required - we reserved 'full-blast' with the windows open for *God save the King, Land of Hope and Glory* and *There'll always be an England,* just to give the locals a treat.

One world event came through from the American station at Schenectady as they were experimenting and seeking the longest range signal. This was the report of the Japanese attack on Pearl Harbour, an event which was to have a dramatic effect on the war - the UK and Commonwealth were no longer alone in the struggle against the Enemy, it was now World War in the fullest sense.

Ron and Fred Soden clearly got on well with the Sivas works employees. So much so, that a number of them wished to learn to speak English. This was communicated to the British Council representative in Turkey, Michael Grant, together with the fact that at Sivas Cement Works there was an engineer, Bey Ahmet Tekant, who had recently graduated with an M.Sc. from London University and was willing to take classes. Ahmet had become engaged to an English girl in Bromley, Kent, and Ron was able to arrange that the earnings for his teaching were sent to her, presumably for saving towards their time together in later years. It was arranged for the British Council to subsidise Tekant's classes, which then commenced. A considerable amount of extra data was also supplied in the form of books and films to encourage these classes. It was all useful in order to build good relations between the countries during the war.

At the end of April Ron was back in Ankara continuing the arrangements for his and Soden's departure from Turkey. Lord Carlisle had arrived back from a diplomatic visit and made the decision that, as there was no trace of the last two locomotives of the 18 which had survived the voyage to Egypt, and he could get no promise of their shipment, the two engineers could start preparing for their departure. The Turkish authorities, in the form of the police department at Sivas, had done nothing towards processing the necessary paperwork to enable exit visas to be issued. Heavy diplomatic pressure from the Embassy through the appropriate Ministry in Ankara finally overcame this lethargic approach.

Suddenly news came through that the two missing '8Fs' were en route from Egypt to Iskenderun and Ron and Fred were asked to defer their departure plans to be able to oversee their completion.

By the end of May 1942, all 18 locomotives that had survived the journey had been erected and most of the wagons were in service, to be found all over the railways of Turkey. Four replacement locomotives were promised for those lost in transit and Ron felt confident enough to leave matters in the hands of the Turkish authorities. On 25th May they left on their journey home from Ankara where they had gone to obtain the exit visas. The previous day a farewell dinner had been given at Sivas works with many of the staff present. Ron had prepared a speech, which he delivered in Turkish to the assembled company.

Fred Soden split up with Ron on the first part of the journey, to make his own way back to Cairo where they were to meet up in a couple of weeks time. Ron travelled as far as Tripoli by train, where he alighted and took a car to Beyrout and then Haifa, arriving there on 30th May. Palestine was an interesting place to visit and Ron took advantage of the few days at his disposal to view several places of interest. From Haifa he made a trip to Nazareth and Tiberius followed by a relaxing afternoon on the shores of the Sea of Galilee, before returning to Haifa. The following day he took a taxi to Tel Aviv and on to Jerusalem where he booked into the Hotel Eden, relishing in the plush comfort of that establishment. Two days were spent exploring Jerusalem before returning to Haifa where he stayed until getting the train for Cairo.

Linking up with Soden at the Hotel Metropolitan, Ron then cabled Riddles asking if a return home by air could be arranged. They were fortunate and an air passage was arranged, with them getting seats in a Short Empire flying boat down the Nile to Lake Albert (Victoria?) and thence across the Congo and up the western coast of Africa to Lagos. Here, after a two day wait they caught a flight back to the UK via the Gambia, Lisbon, Foynes, and thence to Poole Harbour. The aircraft in this case was a Boeing four-engined flying boat. They had been out of the country for 15 months.

The '8Fs' served the Turkish railways for many years, being dubbed 'The Churchills' by the Turks. In 1983, Jim Jarvis visited Turkey and found some still active. Also Sivas works still undertook steam locomotive repairs, although this was shortly to come to an end with the withdrawal of steam in that land.

With his return to England, Ron and May could now start planning for their marriage, which took place on 8th August at St John's Church, Harpenden, with a reception at nearby 'Gorselands'. The weather being unkind, the proceedings planned for the garden had to be transferred to the playroom. The couple spent their first night in a London hotel, after which they departed for a honeymoon in the Scottish Highlands. May resigned from her RCH job on her marriage to devote her time to being a full-time wife to Ron in the house he had recently bought in Littleover near Derby, after it had been thoroughly checked over by his father. The recent overseas experiences seemed a distant memory as he picked up the strands of his railway work on the LMS and settled into a more normal domestic life with May.

The interior of Sivas works in 1983. A German 2-10-0 is under repair.   *J.M. Jarvis*

The wedding, St John's Church, Harpenden, 8th August, 1942.   *Jarvis Collection*

Chapter Five

The Machine Tool Mission to India

Matters in the CME's Department were, in 1942/3, to change somewhat as Stanier had largely devolved his office to C.E. Fairburn, who was now Acting CME, and was more or less full-time as a Scientific Adviser to the Ministry of Production. Fairburn was an electrical engineer by profession and had been quietly establishing his position after Hornbuckle, who ranked equal to him, had resigned at the start of the war. Although Ron still saw Stanier occasionally, it was Fairburn who called the tune in the Design Department.

Once settling back into service at Derby, his duties were largely allied to acting as a go-between from the CME's office at Watford and the Derby design offices. Much travelling between these sites was involved and occasionally he would find himself sharing an official car with Fairburn, who was now based at Derby. In this way he got to know Fairburn quite well, a man who had his own definite views and needed diplomatic handling at times. However, he was not a fit man and could at times be quite irritable. His background had much involvement with electrical matters in the past, and he had been in a high position with the English Electric Company (EE) before being enticed back to the railway scene by Sir Harold Hartley in 1934. Prior to his EE days had been a pupil of Sir Henry Fowler at Derby in Midland Railway days after completing a distinguished three firsts at Oxford, so his grounding in steam was substantial.

One task allocated to Ron in late 1942 was the all-important one of steel allocation for the LMS. This was a complex matter and was, with a lot of hard work, brought to a satisfactory conclusion, ensuring that there were satisfactory supplies of all grades of steel to permit the wartime production and maintenance programmes to be achieved. Ron was particularly proud of this task working out satisfactorily, a task which in peacetime would have been covered by a substantial team.

Before any of the above happened, in fact before his wedding, Ron had received a letter from the BBC Director of Talks. This requested a broadcast at some later date on his experiences in Turkey during wartime. The Ministry of Information had apparently tipped them off on his return to the UK, and it was felt that here was a worthwhile story. Obviously, the LMS had to be approached as to the possibility of allowing this broadcast, but as it concerned locomotives designed by their CME and which were to be seen in service over their lines, the publicity value ensured that clearance was given. Accordingly, Ron wrote a suitable script, which still exists, and the talk was given on the BBC Home Service at 9.20 am on Tuesday 15th December, 1942. This script is to be found in *Appendix One*, and makes interesting reading, particularly as it was clearly edited by the Ministry of Information to make a good picture of what had been a sometimes difficult and diplomatically tense situation. A further broadcast was made later on the BBC Turkish service in which Ron sent greetings to those he and Fred Soden had worked with all those months in Iskenderun and Sivas.

The 'Royal Scot' rebuilds were fine-looking engines. Here No. 6115 *Scots Guardsman* poses ex-works.   *Jarvis Collection*

The final batches of 'Black Fives' had many refinements such as Timken roller bearings, electric lighting equipment, rocking grate, hopper ashpan and self-cleaning smoke boxes. No. 4766 is seen in ex-works condition.   *Jarvis Collection*

This latter was made in Turkish, for Ron had gathered a fair smattering of that language during his protracted stay in that country.

On the home front, as 1942 drew to a close, May informed Ron that their number was to increase next year with the arrival of a baby.

Despite the urgency of the war, there were occasional times of slackness, and Ron filled in his time by embarking on an analysis of the forces acting on the driving axle-boxes of locomotives having two inside cylinders. This showed that, on one side of the engine, a very large horizontal force was created on the bearing, leaving the bearing prone to running hot. The LMS class '4F' 0-6-0 was a case in point as was the Fowler 0-8-0, a situation in both cases being exacerbated by the small bearing area available. The obvious solution was to substitute the boxes for larger ones, but with close on 1,000 engines in service the war effectively prevented this. Further analysis showed that with locomotives having their adjacent inside cranks and outside coupling rod pins in phase, rather than the usual 180 degrees, the forces on the axle-boxes were much reduced. However, apart from producing heavier loads on the crank axle, such a layout called for much heavier balance weights. Some Stroudley locomotives and Great Eastern Railway/LNER class 'B12' 4-6-0s had this latter layout.

Following his return from Turkey, Ron had reopened his regular correspondence with Tommy Hornbuckle, who was now firmly established at the Royal Ordnance Plant near Newcastle. His old chief kept this correspondence going right up until his death in 1958 and it is clear that he had a great respect and confidence in Ron's abilities. With the broadcast and the knowledge of a good job having been achieved in Turkey, Ron's reputation as a first-class engineer was spreading throughout the engineering industries. Several overtures in respect of obtaining his services were made, one in particular coming from SKF, another from the *Railway Gazette*, the latter asking if he would be willing to take on the editorship of their Diesel Supplement in a spare time capacity. Fairburn, having been sounded out on this second request, firmly stated that Ron was not to take on anything outside his already extensive responsibilities for the LMS. All this was mentioned to Hornbuckle in confidence, as he was always a good sounding board for reliable advice where senior management was concerned, viz.: 'Your episode with Ivatt amused me muchly. CDs (Chief Draughtsmen) are very touchy on the point of suggestions affecting design. I annoyed Anderson, Symes and Chambers by such suggestions', as he wrote to Ron at Christmas 1942. The reference to chief draughtsmen was clearly aimed at Tommy Coleman at Derby who resented any design suggestions from outside his own sphere.

The three top persons with whom Ron most came into contact were Stanier, Fairburn and Ivatt. We have already seen that Fairburn needed careful handling, but Ron always had great regard for Stanier and Ivatt, finding them good bosses, approachable and friendly. His and May's high spot in 1943 was the safe arrival of their daughter, Rosemary, in June that year. She was to be their only child.

The war progressed more and more to the favour of the Allies, with the expulsion of the Germans from North Africa and the USA beginning to make severe inroads into the Japanese fleet in the Pacific. Stanier had gained a richly deserved Knighthood and as the Country began to fill with the American armed might and geared up for invasion, preparations were being made for a high-level visit to India by a UK Machine Tool Mission. Sir William was acknowledged as one of the foremost authorities on machine tools in the Country and was to lead the team. Their task was to investigate the condition of India's resources of machine tools, particularly in respect of that employed for aircraft repair and maintenance; aircraft ordnance; ordnance, including carriages, mountings and ammunition; naval and civilian ships; and motor vehicles, locomotives and rolling stock. In addition the team was to advise on the best use of the resources found in order that India could become the first base for the ever increasing operations of South East Asia Command.

Stanier wished to have on hand a reliable engineer to collate all his findings and cast around for a suitable candidate. Ron Jarvis, due to his competent handling of affairs in Turkey and thereafter back at Derby, was chosen to accompany him as personal assistant, the necessary release from his tasks at Derby being cleared with Fairburn. The other members of the Mission were: Mr S.V. Woolley from the Ministry of Supply; Mr B.W. Palmer, Manager of the Railway Department of Messrs G.D. Peters; and Mr W.H.G. Clifton of the Ministry of Aircraft Production.

Preparations went on apace as the Allied forces invaded the French coast in Normandy and, after establishing themselves, began to push inland. The UK Mission departed by air for India by Sunderland flying boat on 20th July, 1944. The journey was to be considerably speedier than that for Turkey in 1941. The first stop was at Gibraltar, where the aircraft was refuelled for the lengthy haul along the Mediterranean to Cairo where they arrived late on the 21st. A short stop of one day was made here. Ron took advantage of looking up the UKCC office and renewing old friendships of the Turkish episode, before taking some of his travelling companions on a brief tour of Cairo and then on to the pyramids.

On the 24th they put down at Bahrain before continuing the following day to Karachi, where their aerial journey finished. The remainder of the outward trip was to be overland to Delhi, where they booked into the Imperial Hotel. The accommodation provided was of the best quality, with suites of rooms for each individual of the Mission. To crown it off, a servant was provided for each of them. Ron had a capable young Indian, Sher Mohammed, who was to be on hand for the whole of his time in India. The days of the Raj had yet to come to a close.

Four days of high-level meetings took place in Delhi with representatives of the Central Government Ministries, covering all industrial aspects to be dealt with during the forthcoming tour. To assist them in the tour, a former CME of the East India Railway, G.A.R. Trimming, who was at that time machine tool controller for India, joined the group.

After concluding their meetings, they were given a conducted tour of Delhi Fort by Sir Archibald Rowlands. This was one of the key places involved in the 1857 Indian Mutiny. The following day they entrained for the 24 hour journey to Calcutta from where they were to start the tour. The Great Eastern Hotel in that city was their abode. Compared to Delhi, Ron found Calcutta noisy and dirty. There was also the disadvantage of a black-out, or rather brown-out, for Japanese bombers still made the occasional raid.

On 2nd August a round of meetings was held in Calcutta with Director Generals of the major industrial concerns to be visited in the East and South of India, together with the representatives of the Machine Tool Control Committee for India. Ron's main responsibility at all meetings was to gather information from the notes taken and collate these into a draft report for Sir William to peruse the next day. Often this task took him well into the late evening, or sometimes early morning, for its completion to his satisfaction. It was a hard grind, but Ron realised that in the sometimes lengthy journeys ahead there would be some time to unwind and relax.

Their mode of transport was Great Indian Peninsular Railway touring carriage, half of which consisted of sleeping accommodation of four two-berth cabins, and the other half a dining and lounge car with a self-contained kitchen. Next to this was coupled a second vehicle, a third class car for the staff of baboos and bearers to serve their needs. These two vehicles were coupled to appropriate express trains or sometimes taken separately on special paths allocated for them as an inspection train.

The first tour took them down the Eastern coastline to Madras and then across the Southern Tamil area to Cochin on the Malabar Coast via Tiruchchirappalli. Cochin appealed to Ron in that the British part of the town was interesting. The church there at one time was the burial place of Vasco da Gama, the Portuguese explorer. There was also a village green there and the whole area was like an English village in a different setting.

From Cochin they travelled up through Mysore and Bangalore before making a special stop at the Nizam's State of Hyderabad from where they returned to Calcutta. The touring coach was used as accommodation at all but the larger towns with acceptable hotels or, as sometimes occurred, guest accommodation of local industries or dignitaries was put at their disposal. One typical example at the start of this tour was a two day stop at the Tata Iron and Steel Works, said to be the largest single plant of its kind in the British Empire, where they were placed in the Director's bungalow guest quarters. They were glad to be able to transfer to these facilities at times, as luxuries such as spacious rooms and baths were available to alleviate the discomfort of the Indian summer heat in a railway carriage. It was also useful to use hotels at locations where visits to several plants had to be made, where sometimes some reciprocal hospitality was appropriate. On one particular occasion, at a hotel, Ron discovered that the baboos were getting into a hopeless mess trying to organise the party's baggage transfer to the station. He intervened, literally at the last minute, and managed to inject some order into the chaos he found, getting the bags to the station just in time and on board just before the train pulled out. This had caused some concern to the party about his time-keeping, the ensuing criticism being neatly deflected by Sir William once he was acquainted of the reason.

There was one particular part of the tour of Southern India in which they left the special carriages and took to the roads. After leaving the coast at Cochin they arrived at Mattapalayan to transfer to a fleet of cars which then took them up into the Nilgiri Hills and to the hill stations of Coonor and Ootacamund. These were at 6,000 feet altitude and the climate much cooler as a result. Ron tended to suffer from prickly heat and this change to the pleasant warmth of the

An East Indian 2-8-0 at Kharagpur after overhaul there; built by Armstrong-Whitworth in 1924.
J.M. Jarvis

Although this class 'HPS2' 4-6-0 was built in 1949, it formed part of a class that dated from the 1920s. Older members of this class probably hauled the trains conveying the Machine Tool Mission at Ranaghat shed near Calcutta.
J.M. Jarvis

hills brought him some welcome relief. The scenery was, according to his description, spectacular. Journeying on by car to Mysore they continued by train to Bhadravati on the metre gauge line in that area. Sixty miles from Bhadravati was Harihar, at which was a machine tool factory on their list. This was reached by a further car journey, and proved to be well laid out and equipped and worthy of encouragement to keep their output going.

A further trip from Bhadravati was to some iron ore mines nearby before returning to the metre gauge train and on to Bangalore, where they arrived in the early morning. There were no meetings that day so, after breakfast, an escorted tour of the nearby Kolah Gold Mines was made. At the mine the party were taken down a 4,800 foot shaft to the workings. This was not as far as the full workings which extended to 7,300 feet. A further extension in depth was planned they were told, which should then make these mines the deepest in the World.

The following day was spent in looking over the Bangalore plant of Hindustan Aircraft Ltd, which was mainly engaged in the repair of American aircraft. Immediately following this factory visit a meeting with the Mysore State Prime Minister took place.

The special train being rejoined after the Bangalore inspections and meeting, the Mission then travelled on to Hyderabad via Madras. Here they stayed as guests of the Nizam of Hyderabad in the Guest House. Ron found time to investigate this city: 'It is a typical old Indian City packed with mosques and bazaars. There is no blackout here and it is all brightly lit at night. We were out until close on midnight last night (9/9/44) foraging through the bazaars . . .'

On 11th September they commenced the final leg of their journey back to Calcutta and the close of the Southern tour. It proved an interesting trip, for the first 60 miles were covered in a railcar, quite a rarity in India, the special coaches having gone on ahead.

To all accounts the time spent in India impressed Ron considerably as to the sights he saw and the people he met: 'This is so far a much more pleasant country than I had expected and it makes me think that Turkey was a hard school', he wrote to May as he journeyed through the varied scenery. The one thing which annoyed him, and the rest of the Mission members, was the inability of the authorities to get their mail through to them. The travelling was so frequent and, at times, to such remote areas that all attempts to get the letters through never actually made it to their location, but seemed to follow them about one or two stops behind. It was some seven weeks after they had been in India that a few letters arrived for them as they returned to Calcutta - a welcome link with home.

A few days rest was taken at Calcutta before the second, and final, tour. This commenced with a visit to Lucknow and a round of the relevant local industries. From here they travelled to Rampur and then on to Lahore. Leaving Lahore for Delhi a brief stop was made at Amritsar to view the Golden Temple, the centre of the Sikh faith: 'The whole place is most ornate but you can imagine that the sunshine makes the temple glisten, and the whole place is really very wonderful', enthused Ron in a letter from Delhi describing the sight of the gold leaf-covered building.

A few days in Delhi sufficed to draft out the report of findings so far, and Sir William made a round of visits to the main bodies interested in the progress of the Mission. The final series of visits were to be made in the Bombay area, but before setting off a short diversion was undertaken to Agra, to enable those in the party who had not seen the Taj Mahal to do so: 'We arrived at Agra at 3.00 am and got up at 4.30 and proceeded to the Taj Mahal in horse-drawn "Tongas". We saw the indescribably beautiful place by moonlight, and then from the top of the main gateway some 400 yards away we watched the sun rise and cast its orange rays obliquely over the great marble Taj', was the description of a never-to-be-forgotten sight penned by Ron to May.

The next suitable train to which to attach their coaches was not until early evening and so further sightseeing was possible. The deserted city of Fatepur Sikri was visited in the morning and in the afternoon Ron detached himself and went back to the Taj Mahal, so enamoured was he with the magnificence of the marble tomb.

In the evening of 8th October the Mission party rejoined their special carriage and set off for Bombay where nearly 10 days on inspection visits were scheduled in the immediate vicinity of that important port and industrial complex. The final factory visit took place on 25th October, following which a brief return visit was made to Poona to relax before the long train journey back to Calcutta. They had been to Poona a few days previously for meetings with the Bombay Government and the place looked interesting, resulting in the second visit. Whilst there Ron met a fellow model railway enthusiast, by the name of Templer, who took him to see some magnificent gauge 'O' models he had made.

Poona and the surrounding area having been digested the long rail journey to Calcutta commenced. Once there they stayed until 2nd November continuing the drafting of their report. The Indian branch of the Institution of Locomotive Engineers entertained them to dinner at the Bengal Club on the 28th and, as the departure date approached, the members of the Mission busied themselves in arranging for the shipment of a large collection of purchases made during the tour.

In these journeys their total travelling covered some 9,000 miles over a three month period, visiting 122 engineering, railway and munition plants. What they had found ranged from the efficient General Motors plant at Howrah to downright chaotic and inefficient operations in some of the smaller Indian-managed concerns, although there was a sprinkling of well-equipped and managed local industries. If India was to become the source of maintenance and supply for the South East Asia Command, a lot needed doing in terms of organisational improvements plus providing adequate modern machine tools of good quality.

Throughout this extensive survey, Ron's task as personal assistant had been to be close to Sir William at all times, noting his comments and observations and preparing a report of each day's business. Sir William was a hard, but fair, taskmaster, expecting the report in his hands first thing the following morning. Also, on the many factory visits his 'big driving wheels', as Ron termed his legs, set a cracking pace for his own much smaller stature!

The cover of the official Report produced after the inspection visits made in India.

Mrs R. Boorne

Whilst the Mission had been in India, events in Europe were moving towards an end. The Allied forces had broken out of the Normandy beach-head and were on course for the German border to be ready for the final onslaught. The pressure on the engineering industries was to begin to slacken the following year and many of the recommendations listed in the Machine Tool Mission final report were only to be partially applied, for the war had less than a year to run.

With the report of their findings written and issued to the Government printing works at Simla, and the series of meetings at an end (some 30 at Government and Local Government level had been organised) the Mission party flew back to the UK, and a rather cooler climate, in November.

Ron returned to Derby and settled in at home with May and Rosemary, who was now 1½ years old and beginning to be more mobile. Her first birthday had taken place as Ron was beginning to prepare for the Indian trip and she certainly seemed to have grown a lot during his absence.

The exchange of letters with Tommy Hornbuckle restarted soon after his return and, in one written on 15th December, 1944, to Ron, the following comment appears: 'I am sure that the trip has been a most valuable experience for you and I have no doubt that you did the work extremely well'. The work certainly had been arduous, in a hot and humid climate, but the recognition from such as Hornbuckle gave Ron quiet satisfaction that his efforts were not in vain.

In 1944, a proposal was made to use manganese steel, noted for its work-hardening qualities and thus capable of hard wear, for the flat fore and aft guide surfaces of locomotive axle-boxes. Initially, Fairburn authorised the fitting of

INTRODUCTION.

1. A number of reports have been made on various phases of India's requirements for machine tools in connection with Government schemes for the expansion of the armament programmes for the War Effort.

His Majesty's Government and the Government of India decided that a further review was desirable and the Minister of Supply made arrangements for a U. K. Machine Tool Utilization Committee to visit India with specific terms of reference.

Many of the Ordnance projects had been put forward, at a time when the dispersal of manufacturing plants at home and abroad was essential; and in addition, there was the growing need of improving the facilities in India. Further, the increase in the number of aeroplanes sent to the East, with the difficulty of supplying spares, made it imperative that some provision should be made so that if necessary tools and spare parts could be manufactured in India.

With the change in programmes and the progress of the war in the West, the question of the supply of machine tools on old orders and new requisitions should be reviewed.

COMPOSITION OF THE MISSION.

2. The Minister of Supply appointed the following to be members of the Mission :

Chairman :—
Sir William A. Stanier, F.R.S., M.I.Mech.E., M.I.Loco.E.

Members :—
Mr. S. V. Woolley, M.I.Mech.E., M.I.Prod.E., Machine Tool Control, Ministry of Supply.
Mr. B. W. Palmer, M.I.Loco.E., Manager of Railway Department, Messrs. G. D. Peters, Nr. Slough.
Mr. W. H. G. Clifton, Production Engineer, Ministry of Aircraft Production.
Mr. R. G. Jarvis, B.Sc. (Eng.), A.M.I.Mech.E., from British Railways Staff.

TERMS OF REFERENCE.

3. To take stock of India's resources of Engineering Plant and Machine Tools, with particular reference to the repair and maintenance of the following items :—
(a) Aircraft and Aircraft Ordnance.
(b) Ordnance including Carriages, Mountings and Ammunition.
(c) Naval and Civilian Ships.
(d) Motor Transport Vehicles.
(e) Locomotives and Rolling Stock.
To advise on the best use thereof for the purpose of carrying out objective of making India the first base for operations by South East Asia Command.
To recommend such adjustments of the distribution of machine tools as may be considered desirable and to suggest measures for their improved utilization.
L44ISD(64)

APPENDIX I.

Meetings held with representatives of Central and Provincial Governments, Chambers of Commerce, Industrial Organisations, etc.

Date		Held at
July 26th	War Transport Department	Delhi
July 26th	Hon'ble Member for Supply	Delhi
July 26th	Secretary, Department of Supply	Delhi
July 27th	Eastern Group Supply Council, U.K. Representatives	Delhi
July 27th	Postwar Development Committee	Delhi
July 28th	Railway Board	Delhi
July 28th	Controller of Standards Rly. Board	Delhi
July 28th	Postwar Development Representative, Railway Board	Delhi
July 29th	Master General of Ordnance	Delhi
Aug. 2nd	Director General Munitions Production	Calcutta
Aug. 2nd	Director General Ship-building & Repairs	Calcutta
Aug. 2nd	Director General of Aircraft	Calcutta
Aug. 2nd	Machine Tool Control	Calcutta
Aug. 2nd	Members of Machine Tool Advisory Panel	Calcutta
Aug. 15th	Full Committee, Machine Tool Advisory Panel	Calcutta
Aug. 15th	Engineering Association of India	Calcutta
Aug. 15th	Members of the Bengal Government	Calcutta
Aug. 18th	Directors of Messrs. Tatas	Jamshedpur
Aug. 23rd	Adviser to Government of Madras	Madras
Aug. 24th	Madras Chamber of Commerce	Madras
Aug. 24th	South Indian Chamber of Commerce	Madras
Aug. 24th	Andhra Indian Chamber of Commerce	Madras
Aug. 24th	Tamil Indian Chamber of Commerce	Madras
Aug. 24th	Muslim Indian Chamber of Commerce	Madras
Aug. 24th	South Indian Film Chamber of Commerce	Madras
Sep. 4th	Representative of Mysore Industries	Bangalore
Sep. 4th	Dewan, Mysore State	Bangalore
Sep. 5th	Indian Institute of Science	Bangalore
Sep. 8th	Managing Director, H.E.H. the Nizam's State Railway	Secunderabad
Sep. 8th	Finance Minister, H.E.H. the Nizam's Government	Hyderabad
Sep. 9th	Secretary, Department of Supply	Calcutta
Sep. 24th	Secretary, Department of Supply & Chief Maintenance Officer, R.A.F. India Command	Lucknow
Sep. 25th	Members of U.P. Government	Lucknow
Sep. 27th	Government of Rampur State & Directors of Messrs. Govan Bros.	*Rampur
Oct. 11th	Representative of the Punjab Government	Lahore
Oct. 11th	Bombay Chamber of Commerce	Bombay
Oct. 11th	All-Indian Muslim Chamber of Commerce & Industry	Bombay
Oct. 11th	Mill Owners' Association	Bombay
Oct. 16th	Indian Merchants' Chamber	Bombay
Oct. 16th	Representatives of Messrs. Tatas	Bombay
Oct. 19th	Representatives of Bombay Government	Poona

L44ISD(64)

Left: First page of Machine Tool Mission report. *Right:* The itinerary of meetings held throughout India by the Machine Tool Mission. *Mrs R. Boorne*

five class '5' 4-6-0 engines built at Derby in November-December 1944. These were Nos. 4817-20, 23. These went into service and were monitored every 10,000 miles by dropping the rear wheels. After two examinations it was obvious that the wear was much less than with the previous material used.

By the end of 1945 a decision was taken to fit all new engines of other classes with the manganese steel liners and modify all the class '5s' at each major repair. The net result was to eliminate one of the two intermediate repairs normally carried out between the general overhauls and leading to reduced maintenance costs. Ron, in his later job of overseeing the inspection of locomotives and stock, collected together the available information on those with manganese liners and compared this with that for the unmodified examples. The outcome was shown to be a total saving of £1,100 per engine over a complete maintenance cycle - major repair to major repair. This, at a time when the railways were recovering from the rigours of wartime excess and were trying to trim their running costs, was most welcome.

Chapter Six

A Middle East visit and Nationalisation

As the war ended, with last year's Indian experience behind him, Ron began to settle back into involvement in the many engineering tasks facing the LMS CME's Department at Derby. Matters at the top of that department were in a bit of turmoil, as Fairburn, never a very fit man, died suddenly at the end of 1945. Ivatt was his Principal Assistant and deputy CME, and immediately took over on a temporary basis. On grounds of seniority and experience, he should have been appointed CME straight away, but the LMS Board, influenced somewhat by Sir Harold Hartley, an academic as Fairburn had been, seemed to hesitate about making the temporary appointment permanent. Ron had acquired a good rapport with Sir William Stanier, particularly over the Indian association, and sent a note to his former chief in support of Ivatt. Although now retired from the LMS, Stanier clearly held considerable sway with the Board, for following his backing for Ivatt, they accorded him the CME's position. As Sir William mentioned to Ron some time shortly after the event: 'You nearly didn't get him'.

George Ivatt was, according to Ron, one of the two best Chiefs under whom he worked, Stanier being the other. Appearing to be 'laid back' to those outside the CME's Department, Ivatt was, in fact, a first-class engineer whose extensive knowledge of steam locomotives extended to more modern motive power units. His planning and powers of persuasion in relation to the latter were to bring about the first serious application of diesel-electric locomotives for main-line use on the UK railways.

An immensely practical man, Ivatt realised that the state of much of the stock, locomotives, carriages and wagons, left much to be desired following heavy use and minimal maintenance during the war. Much needed to be done to pin down the causes of 'awaiting and under repair' of a proportion of a fleet of some 7,600 locomotives. There was a need for a small team of technically qualified mechanical inspectors in the CME's Department, which was duly set up in 1946, Ron Jarvis being appointed its first Chief.

Ron's remit was to track down and investigate problems on locomotives in service. Locating, listing and analysing these should, it was reasoned, lead to improvements in detail design and maintenance practices, as well as monitoring new classes entering service or the performance of experimental fittings. As a result of this, some typical improvements involved modified arrangements for under-slung axle-box springs and horn-stays; the benefit of manganese steel liners on axle-boxes; failures of middle big ends of 3-cylinder locomotives were reduced; rough-riding characteristics alleviated by improved valve settings plus many others. This new office was able to concentrate on these problems in a thorough way and certainly much quicker than by using the reports emanating from the Motive Power Superintendent's Department.

Almost immediately after settling into his new position, Ivatt began designing two small locomotives, a 2-6-0 plus a 2-6-2T. Both were in service by 1946 and were

In 1946, Ron's parents celebrated their 40th Wedding anniversary. Here is a group photograph of the whole family taken at that event. *Left to right* we have: Jim, Jessie (Geoffrey's wife), Heather, Jackie (Geoffrey's daughter), father, mother, Geoffrey, Rosemary, May, Ron.

J.M. Jarvis

The jet engine snow-blowing experiment in early 1947, a joint LMS/Rolls Royce venture. Ron Jarvis is in the right foreground   *R.G. Jarvis Collection*

intended to replace sundry pre-Grouping types such as MR 0-4-4Ts, LNWR 2-4-2Ts and 0-6-2Ts which had been displaced to lesser passenger and branch line work, as well as other pre-Grouping small tender types now obsolescent.

The Stanier 2-8-0s, of which some were being returned to the UK following overseas war service, also came in for some attention. One item in particular being pushed Ron's way was the need to ease the workload on this engine when dropping the fire for washouts. Firstly, a rocking grate was installed, but the shape of the ash-pan on the 2-8-0 was such that it was difficult to extract the remains of the fire due to the position of the third coupled axle in front of the forward damper door. This problem came to the CME's Inspection Department, and Ron cast his mind back to the days in Turkey where he had had the chance to inspect the German 2-10-0s operating there. These locomotives employed ash-pans with the bottom comprising a series of centrally-pivoted slats. These were linked together and turned through 90 degrees by a simple lever and enabled the ash to be discharged in one operation. Ivatt immediately saw the simplicity of this and, in conjunction with the rocking grate, it proved possible to reduce the time taken at a shed to drop a fire and clear the ashpan from 35 minutes to just five minutes.

Ron had a small team, no more than four, to fulfil his tasks. A good sign that things were under way was a number of empty desks in the Nelson Street office.

Much of the remedial aspects of the above involved close liaison with the locomotive drawing office. The chief draughtsman at that time was still Tommy Coleman, who had been plucked from his Horwich position by Stanier when building up his team in the early 1930s. Coleman, a very capable Chief, ran his office firmly and was somewhat of a rough diamond. As we have already seen, he tended to resent proposals for changes or improvements from outside his immediate department and clearly needed diplomatic handling. Bluff and outspoken he may have been, he was a shrewd designer, and recognised in Ron's unflappable direct manner a first-class engineer, and could usually be persuaded to adopt the suggested changes.

In 1948 Ron was much involved in matters associated with locomotive testing at Derby which got him serving on an *ad hoc* Locomotive Testing Committee chaired by E.S. Cox. The committee was made up of those most closely connected with locomotive performance and testing on the different Regions of the newly set up British Railways. It was thought that he might be in the running for the officer to be put in charge of the new Loco Testing facility at Rugby, but this was not to be. As Hornbuckle wrote to him shortly after learning that Ron was not to get that position: 'I was very pleased to hear that you were passed over for the Locomotive Testing Plant, I am certain it would have been no good to you. Design and development is your line . . .'

Together with his interest in railway photography, Ron retained a strong desire to influence the preservation scene. In Stanier's day this had not been a good subject to bring up with his superiors, for Stanier showed little interest in preserving historic locomotives as witness the 1932 episode of having some carefully restored Midland and North London (NLR) types cut up at Derby, with only the old Johnson single being saved for posterity. In those days Ron

A rather grimy 'Black Five', No. 4866, on a train resistance test, one of the many programmes involving Ron in the days after the war.   *R.G. Jarvis Collection*

LMS No. 20002, a Kirtley design, which somehow escaped the scrapping net, seen after overhaul at Derby, 31st January, 1935.   *R.G. Jarvis*

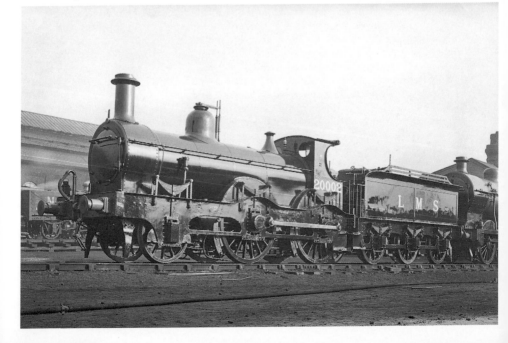

was still very junior and did not have any access to high authority. Now, in 1946, he had the attention of Ivatt who was interested in matters historical. One little job which Ivatt requested in early 1947 was for Ron to visit the main LMS works to ascertain what documents, drawings and other items (this latter encompassing locomotives) of historical interest were still around.

Ron accordingly visited Crewe, Horwich and St Rollox for a preliminary survey. At Crewe he found drawings from as far back as the 1840s. These were of immense historic value, having been made by F.W. Webb and signed by Trevithick and Ramsbottom. Also at Crewe were a number of early drawings originating from private manufacturers. Horwich, being the newest of the works (built 1888) had nothing before 1890 and, at St Rollox only general arrangements of Caledonian stock from 1860 had been kept. Derby drawings before 1874 had long since been destroyed.

Having located such drawings as still existed, and realising their historic value, Ron made strong representations to Ivatt that these should be collected together from the various drawing offices and retained securely at Derby. Ivatt agreed to this, and a special lockable drawing chest was made and placed in Ivatt's office into which the historic artefacts were then stored. It was fortuitous that these were all collected together at that time, before any general 'clear-out' was made, and the historic archives now at the National Railway Museum (NRM) were eventually to benefit from the transfer of many of these drawings saved at Ron's instigation.

On the photographic side the findings were mixed, with nothing at St Rollox and the Crewe and Derby collections of glass negatives retained at Derby. Horwich just had photographic albums covering all the Lancashire and Yorkshire stock. The St Rollox story was a sad one, as the entire collection of glass negatives were smashed whilst being delivered back to the works, the parcel containing them being carelessly thrown from a moving train onto the station platform.

As regards locomotives, the NLR 4-4-0T, a MR 0-4-4T, MR 2-4-0 No. 1, and MR 0-6-0, the latter two both Kirtley double-framers, had gone in Stanier's edict of 1932 with, as we have seen, only the Johnson single surviving. However, in July 1947 LMS No. 20002, formerly MR No. 2, was withdrawn and when Ivatt was acquainted of this by Ron he decided that the 81-year-old veteran 2-4-0 merited preservation, despite the fact that, in Ron's own words: 'This was against the advice of other officials, who opined that the loco was of no special interest historically. Circumstances enabled me to include the loco in the Exhibition held at Chesterfield to celebrate the centenary of George Stephenson's death, after which it became, more or less, a preserved loco.' Also, up at St Rollox stood two rusting and cannibalised locomotives, Caledonian single No. 123 and the old Highland 4-6-0, or 'Jones Goods'. These latter two had been saved in 1935, apparently at the request of the LMS Scottish Board.

Once Ron had let the CME know of the St Rollox pair, Ivatt authorised their restoration to working order and preservation. So, at last, some progress was being made to keep examples of historic locomotives for museum exhibits. In fact the Caledonian single went back into limited service and was, in later years, the last single-driver to operate scheduled runs on BR. The 'Jones Goods' served

Rebuilt 'Royal Scot' No. 46120 *Royal Inniskilling Fusilier* on a flange-force test train at Peak Forest Junction, Derbyshire.   *R.G. Jarvis Collection*

The LMS mobile test train prepared for departure on a test run. Note the special tender fitted to class '5' No. 44764.   *R.G. Jarvis Collection*

for many years on specials and was used for the occasional film work needing an historic engine. Both locomotives are now in honourable retirement in Glasgow Museum of Transport.

The legacy of Ron's consistent and, latterly successful, attempts at preservation of historic locomotives subsequently ensured that some further examples were laid aside for posterity. In September 1951 one of the first two Midland Compounds to be built in 1901 was scheduled for withdrawal. Instead of being cut up, this locomotive sat in storage sidings at Derby and Crewe for eventual restoration to the condition as rebuilt in 1914, given the number 1000 and made available for service on specials until the end of 1959, before being delivered to the Clapham Museum of British Transport. It now resides in the NRM at York as part of the National Collection.

A further classic design preserved was an example of the London, Tilbury & Southend Railway (LT&SR) 4-4-2T, No. 41966, which was put through Derby works in 1956 and given its original No. 80 and name *Thundersley* ready for the LT&SR Centenary celebrations. This too became part of the National Collection and is, at the time of writing, at the Bressingham Steam Museum in Norfolk.

1947 was notable for the extremely severe winter as the year opened. The heavy snowfalls produced conditions where the drifting snow blocked many main and branch lines and threatened to bring much more of the LMS to a halt. Ron could not help thinking back to similar conditions he had experienced in Turkey some five years earlier whilst endeavouring to arrange the transport of the '8F' parts up into the wild, cold Anatolian highlands around Sivas.

The LMS and Rolls-Royce, in a bid to produce some means of clearing deep drifts from blocked lines, collaborated on a novel scheme, that of using the exhaust of jet engines to blast away the snow. Rolls-Royce provided two Derwent jet engines which were mounted on a suitably modified container flat wagon which itself was coupled to a 400 gallon tank wagon holding the fuel supply. A brake van was interposed between this assembly and the '3F' 0-6-0 used for propulsion. The initial line chosen for the first experiment was that from Ashbourne to Buxton, where, at one point, a 14 ft drift had built up. This was followed up by several other trials on other lines, Ron being in attendance on some of them. Whilst capable of clearing newly fallen snow in a spectacular fashion, this apparatus failed miserably with hard-packed drifts, merely boring a hole through the consolidated snow. Care also needed to be taken that the exhaust pipes were not rammed into the snow. This novel experiment was quietly side-lined and no firm plans were made to further it.

Following these disappointing trials, some limited work was done on more conventional methods. Ron cast his mind back to the Turkish episode, remembering that the '8Fs' delivered there had been fitted with cow-catchers, designed by the North British Locomotive Company (NBL), which had proved useful, when fitted with covering sheets, for clearing tracks of limited amounts of small snow depths. Although the LMS had snow ploughs capable of being fitted to several classes of locomotive, these protruded beyond the buffers and were prone to damage on shunting operations or in sheds. The NBL design did not protrude that far and he was of the opinion that the design could be modified into a snow-plough, and accordingly arranged for NBL to supply two

'8F' No. 70507 (WD) at 199 Railway Workshops, Jaffa, Palestine in the Summer of 1947 after completion of intermediate overhaul.   *D. Stewart Currie*

Also found in Palestine was this import from China (ex-Canton Kowloon Railway) as WD No. 70219.   *R.G. Jarvis Collection*

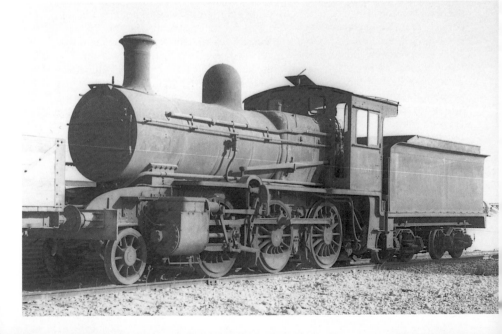

sets of drawings to Derby. A number of ploughs based on this information were built and fitted to '8F' 2-8-0s and '5F' 2-6-0s for operation over Ais Gill between late autumn and early spring.

As the war had run down in the Middle East, a large number of '8F' 2-8-0s supplied there had, after much use, been withdrawn and stored at Royal Engineer's (RE) depots in Palestine and Egypt. Technically, they were still the property of the War Department and moves were being made to assess whether their condition warranted purchase and return to the UK, where motive power needed bolstering after the war. Before any shipping plans could be made, some report on their condition was needed. Ron was accordingly delegated to go out and inspect the stored locomotives and recommend which were mechanically sound enough to return to their home country. His experience in Turkey would prove useful in this task of retrieving batches of useful locomotives.

Initially, in September 1947, Ron travelled to Palestine, to the 199 Railway Workshop at Jaffa where some '8Fs' were in storage. Most of these had served on the Trans-Iranian Railway conveying supplies to Russia. They were eventually superseded by larger, more powerful, American 2-8-2s and gradually withdrawn and placed in storage until the war ended. Eventually 71 of the 93 remaining in Iran were taken from Basra to Baghdad over the metre gauge line on specially-constructed bogies. Twelve of these were left in Iraq and the balance travelled over the standard gauge track via Syria and Palestine to Jaffa and Suez, where there were extensive RE depots. From Jaffa he made a few visits to this depot's sidings at Akhziv, near the Lebanese border. He was glad when this latter assignation was over, as the situation in Palestine leading up to the end of the British Mandate in May 1948 was dangerous, with Jewish terrorists liable to attack Britons found in what was to become their State in the near future. An armed escort was provided for all these jaunts to the sidings.

Following his few days in Palestine, Ron then travelled to 169 Railway Workshops in Suez, where another clutch of ex-Iranian '8Fs' were stored, to complete his round of inspections. This journey was made on the Haifa to Cairo Express, with a change at Ismailia for Suez. He was met at Suez by Lt D. Stewart Currie of the Royal Engineers and installed in the Guest Tent at 169 Rly W/S. He messed with Lt Currie and the other six officers, only griping a bit about the need to change from his overalls into more presentable clothing for lunchtime in the mess. The local environment was decidedly more friendly than Palestine and the workshops certainly appeared to be dedicated to engineering operations and military discipline was minimal in its interference with matters in hand.

As in Palestine, some of these '8Fs' were deemed satisfactory for a return to the UK and, after overhaul, a return to service for some 39 engines, plus four spare tenders, was feasible on what would then be British Railways. Arrangements were put in hand for this. By the end of October, Ron was back at Derby, taking up the running of his department.

The 39 locomotives were shipped back in April and May of 1948 to be given a complete overhaul, which included the removal of the oil burning equipment fitted, and entered service on BR. The first 20 comprised the entire cargo of the SS *Belnor*, a Norwegian ship which had a derrick capable of lifting 90 tons. Each

The Officers Mess at 169 Rly W/S, Suez: ante room and bar to the left, and kitchen and dining room at the rear. The roof was provided from a pair of USA bogie wagon roofs.

D. Stewart Currie

A general view of 169 Rly W/S, where the '8Fs' were overhauled.   *D. Stewart Currie*

'8F' locomotives in 400 Transportation Stores Dept, Suez, awaiting inspection by Ron Jarvis in October 1947. This batch had been serving in Iraq up to the end of 1945 before being stored in Palestine and eventually moved to Egypt.   *D. Stewart Currie*

Retained at Suez was a strategic reserve of '8Fs'. This photograph depicts a line of them.
                    R.G. Jarvis Collection

'8F' locomotive No. 41-135 (WD) at 169 Rly W/S. Note the extra water tanker (4,000 gallons) coupled to the locomotive. *D. Stewart Currie*

Some of the '8Fs' inspected by Ron were missing many parts and were considered unworthy of return to the UK. *R.G. Jarvis Collection*

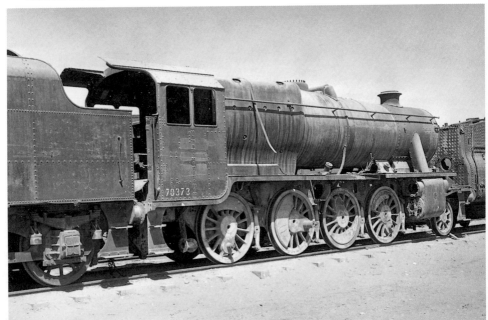

'8F' No. 70395 sets off for Port Said, with three others in tow, for repatriation in April 1948.
D. Stewart Currie

The 150 ton capacity crane belonging to the Suez Canal Co. lifting an '8F' locomotive onto a barge in order to take it out to the SS *Belnor*.   *D. Stewart Currie*

Lifting one of the '8Fs' onto the SS *Belnor*. The 70 tons of the locomotive causes the 11 degree list.
D. Stewart Currie

SS *Belnor* lifting one of the '8Fs' on board using the ship's jumbo derrick.   *D. Stewart Currie*

The SS *Belnor* with 20 locomotives and tenders loaded and ready to sail.
D. Stewart Currie

locomotive was transhipped to the *Belnor* on a modified landing craft and lifted onto the vessel by the derrick. The initial hoist of some 70 tons produced an 11 degree list on the ship until the load was swung inboard for stowage.

As with many of the unusual assignments over the years, an account of the Middle Eastern trip was put in a letter to Hornbuckle, who replied on 28th October, 1948 in the usual congratulatory vein: 'Very pleased to hear of your trip to Egypt and Palestine. These excursions not only break the tedium of everyday routine but are such useful experience. They are also evidence of confidence in your judgement.'

Also, in May 1948, Ron, in company with Tom Coleman, visited the premises of the Swiss Locomotive and Machine Works (SLM) at Winterthur, Switzerland, to discuss the possibility of BR using rotary snow ploughs to improve on the current locomotive pusher ploughs. They came back with a series of proposals for the acquisition of one or two rotary snow ploughs based on the Swiss models and communicated this to Ivatt on 11th June, 1948. Ivatt took a few weeks to come to a decision and on 23rd August sent a letter to R.A. Riddles, in charge of locomotive matters at the Railway Executive, recommending that two units should be constructed using snow clearing rotors built in Switzerland. These would be mounted on purpose-built chassis carrying a standard steam locomotive boiler and cylinders to provide the necessary power for driving the rotors. However, as far as can be ascertained, no order was ever placed. The contacts made on this initial trip to were, in later years, most helpful in the negotiations covering design features developed at the SLM works and adopted for use on later British Railways designs for electric and electro-diesel locomotives when Ron was at Brighton.

Two of the 'Jintys' that were found at Savenay in France having survived the war years on the French Railways under the German occupation.   *R.G. Jarvis Collection*

Despite its careworn look this 'Jinty' was returned to the UK and rebuilt to give several more years service.   *R.G. Jarvis Collection*

One further overseas assignment for Ron came in 1948, when he travelled to France to inspect a batch of ex-LMS '3F' 0-6-0Ts, built under Fowler. These had been requisitioned by the War Department in early 1940, and eight examples shipped to France for use by the British Expeditionary Force. However, the rapid advance of the Germans meant there was no chance of repatriating them and they were left behind, being absorbed into the French Railways. Five had survived the rigours of the war and awaited a return to the UK. Of the other three there was no sign and it is thought that they were damaged and scrapped as a result of air raids. The five '3Fs' located were shipped back to England and, following a thorough overhaul at Derby, were replaced in the BR stock to serve out their lives on shunting and minor duties.

It was between April and September of 1948 that the British Railways Interchange Trials of locomotives from the various Regions were carried out. These trials were not as comprehensive as many would have liked, as for the Regions involved there were only three dynamometer cars available. Also loading gauge restrictions and crews refusing to work lodging turns made matters difficult for the organisers. A committee was set up to collate all the results into a final report for the Railway Executive. This consisted of:

Ron Jarvis	for the London Midland Region
S.O. Ell	for the Western Region
C.S. Cocks	for the Southern Region
B. Spencer	for the Eastern and North Eastern Regions

Riddles returned to the LMS at the end of the war and was appointed a Vice-President in 1946. Before the Nationalisation programme started in 1948, he was selected to build up an engineering team at the Marylebone HQ to oversee all the Regional Departments and decide the policy of such matters for BR as a whole. He was also a Chief much respected by Ron and his earlier close liaison with Sir William Stanier had ensured that many engineering decisions to emanate from his directives were sound. He was one of those Chief Engineers who was always very good in paying visits to the drawing offices and discussing the problems with the men on the boards.

One of Riddles first calls on the senior staff at Derby was for E.S. Cox to join him as Executive Officer (Design). Cox had, up to then, been Chief Technical Assistant to Ivatt who was now Chief Mechanical and Electrical Engineer for the London Midland Region of BR. Ron was promoted to the post vacated by Cox and began a time of close association with Ivatt, who was very busy seeing his larger 2-6-0s into production to replace some of the older types being withdrawn.

There was much to be done with Ivatt as the new small 2-6-0s and 2-6-2Ts were being built and entering service. These small, but useful locomotives were being supplemented by the new, larger, 2-6-0 which, as Nationalisation got under way, was entering production. These three classes of Ivatt were, eventually, with sundry slight modifications, to become three of the 11 standard BR designs shortly to be drawn up by Riddles and Bond.

Additionally, Ivatt was much engrossed in the trials of the two prototype diesel-electrics Nos. 10000 and 10001. These had entered traffic in early 1948 and

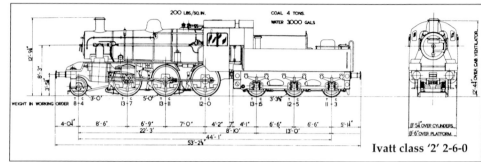

Ivatt class '2' 2-6-0

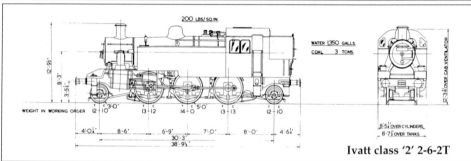

Ivatt class '2' 2-6-2T

The year before Ron moved to Brighton, his father and sister Heather flew to Nice for a holiday. On landing, the aircraft failed to stop and ran off the end of the runway and ended up as shown. The type involved is an Air France 'Languedoc'.   *J.M. Jarvis*

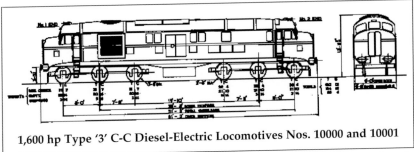

1,600 hp Type '3' C-C Diesel-Electric Locomotives Nos. 10000 and 10001

were proving very capable and reliable units, fully vindicating Ivatt's predictions of being good substitutes for steam locomotives. Riddles, however, was primarily a steam man and continued to plan for the range of standard steam locomotives, even with the potential of diesel-electric there for all to see. The big drawback was clearly the capital cost of this new form of power when compared to an equivalent steam type. Perhaps had more emphasis been put on the immediacy and ease of preparation of such units, with the attendant cost reductions, the argument may have gone the other way. However, the appearance of Nos. 10000 and 10001 had stung the other railways into action. The SR had begun to design its own diesel-electric whilst the GWR had entered the fray with a prototype gas turbine design purchased from Switzerland. The LNER had expanded its trans-Pennine electrified line and was using a fleet of 1,740 hp Bo-Bo electric locomotives on freight traffic over that route.

After two years of BR's existence the many design teams absorbed from the four railways were still much engaged on designs based on the stock produced by them prior to Nationalisation. Apart from unnecessary duplication of effort this hardly assisted the daunting task of developing a range of standard locomotives and rolling stock. Riddles was now firmly in overall charge at BR Headquarters and delegated Cox to co-ordinate the necessary tasks at four main centres, Derby, Doncaster, Swindon and Brighton. A cross-posting of key management staff was inaugurated to ensure the spread of design philosophies from one area to another. Consequently Ron found himself preparing for a move to Brighton, which had already been given the task of designing for production two of the eventual standard types. The job was a challenging one, to the position of Chief Technical Assistant, CM&EE Department, Southern Region, where he would be in charge of all the design offices on that Region.

He had been at Derby, on and off, since those early apprenticeship days commencing in 1928 and was well known around the works and offices. His colleagues at the Nelson Street offices determined that he would not leave without some form of reminder of his Derby years and arranged a presentation gathering to bid him farewell. They delegated one of their number, George Fisher, a clock expert, to obtain a suitable clock as a gift from themselves. He returned from Sheffield with a rather flamboyant example which all his colleagues thought would not suit straight-laced Ron. George tried again and brought back a far more suitable example of a carriage clock, which was much appreciated by both Ron and May.

Brighton Works: Atlantic No. 32421 undergoes some repairs.   *Jarvis Collection*

The only 'Leader' to run on trials, No. 36001, poses at Fratton on 6th June, 1950.   *R.G. Jarvis*

Chapter Seven

Brighton Days,
The 'Leader' and two Class '4s'

At last, the opportunity to be in charge of a sizeable organisation with responsibility for day-to-day running of a complete design and development team was on Ron's plate. Two years previously, Tommy Hornbuckle had commented in one of his regular letters: 'Design and development is your line for some time to come'.

Now, upon his starting at Brighton, a further encouraging note from Hornbuckle arrived: 'Today you will be starting on your new duties and I wish you the best of luck. I am sure you are extremely fortunate in being transferred to the Southern. Bulleid had bold ideas and the present chief (Warder) is an electrical man. The conditions are extremely favourable to your development.'

O.V.S. Bulleid, the former CME of the Southern Railway had, in his decade in that position, begun to introduce a range of new locomotives incorporating some new features in detail design. Ron was to find himself embroiled in three of those types involving the radical approach of Bulleid. Two of these were the 'Merchant Navy' and 'West Country' Pacifics, of which there were some 135 in service, 30 of the former and 105 of the latter, with a final batch of five of the 'West Country' class being erected at Brighton. The third type was a complete departure from the norm so far as locomotives went, the 0-6-6-0T 'Leader' class. Of this latter a prototype was being tested and a batch of four more were in various stages of construction as Ron took over the design offices.

This last design of Bulleid stemmed from the need to replace the ageing 'M7' 0-4-4Ts of Drummond, designed in 1897, of which there were 104 in service over the Southern Region. Studies had been commenced in 1945 at the Brighton office and by April 1946 the 0-6-6-0 double bogie layout was selected. Design studies continued and on 11th September, 1946 the drawing office received Order No. 3382: 'Build five tank engines to Diagram W7326'.

The final design incorporated a range of novel and radical proposals, these being:

(a) The incorporation of the engine units on the bogies themselves.
(b) No coupling rods, but all axles chain driven from the central, powered, axle.
(c) The valve gear consisted of sleeve valves operated by valve motion driven from a sprocket on the driving axle.
(d) The driver to have a cab at either end of the locomotive body.
(e) The boiler to be offset to permit access through the locomotive from one cab to the other.
(f) A dry-sided firebox of all-welded construction (as was the boiler) to be employed.
(g) No fewer than four thermic syphons installed in the firebox to provide a large heating area.
(h) The fireman's station in the centre of the locomotive between the firebox and fuel and water storage.

However, it should be mentioned that items (e) and (h) were there by default, for Bulleid's original design was based on oilfiring, with the fireman

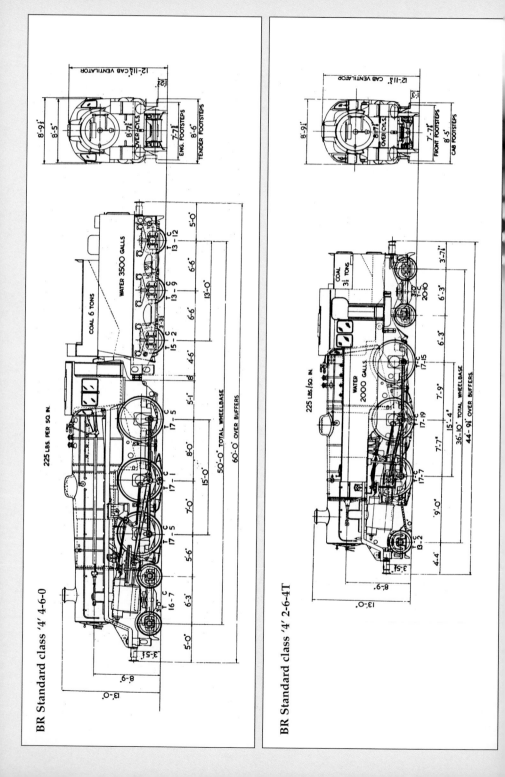

BR Standard class '4' 4-6-0

BR Standard class '4' 2-6-4T

accompanying the driver in the end cab. This was forestalled by the shortage of oil following the war, which resulted in the Southern Locomotive Committee vetoing oilfiring. The need to revert to coal firing meant that the fireman needed to be positioned by the firebox. The offset boiler was dictated by the communication passage between driver and fireman stations.

Matters moved slowly at the start and it was not until July 1947 that construction of the prototype began. It was realised at the start that the sleeve valves might prove difficult to develop and wisely it was decided to try out the concept on a 'guinea-pig' locomotive. This decision was reinforced by the knowledge of the problems found on the ill-starred Paget 2-6-2 design of 1905 which had also included sleeve valves. The locomotive chosen for the trial was a Marsh class 'H1' 4-4-2 then approaching the end of its useful life. By November 1947 this had been converted and steamed for the first time. It was not until March the following year that some intermittent local runs were made, which terminated in June. Not much happened until March 1949, when a few runs in service were initiated, culminating in a return to the works in June. Several failures had occurred and the difficulty of maintaining steam tightness around the sleeve valves was all too evident. The locomotive when in service appeared to be shrouded in steam at the front end.

Despite the obvious drawbacks shown by excessive steam leakage, construction of the prototype 'Leader' continued unchanged. The main frames were completed in May 1948, but the locomotive itself was not finished until June 1949. By now British Railways was well-established and Robert Riddles was now effectively the CME overseeing all Regional locomotive developments from headquarters.

The position of Chief Technical Assistant at Brighton brought the drawing offices at Brighton, Eastleigh and Ashford under Ron's control. The Brighton office had 28 permanent staff plus three trainees and was shortly to be engaged on the preparation of the detail design of the BR Standard 2-6-4T and 4-6-0 locomotives of power class '4'. A small section dealt with modifications to the prototype 'Leader'. A considerable amount of effort was also being made into modifications to the Bulleid Pacifics to alleviate problems allied to serviceability of these types, which was costing a lot in poor availability.

Brighton was a relatively small, but very capable, works. About 600 were employed in the technical and production facilities. It had been rescued from almost certain closure by World War II demands for all available production space, and was capable of erecting considerable numbers of medium and large locomotives. The principle employed by the Southern Region was to manufacture the parts mainly at Ashford and Eastleigh according to their respective capabilities at any given time, with Brighton manufacturing those parts which they were unable to undertake. Any repairs to the older ex-London, Brighton & South Coast Railway designs were also covered at Brighton.

Bulleid, who had retired in 1949, had let staffing matters slide at the end of his career, and several experienced men had left for jobs elsewhere. A general air of low morale was apparent and Ron speedily assessed the needs in a memo to S.B. Warder at Regional Headquarters and arranged that the ongoing work on modifications to the Bulleid Pacifics be transferred to the Eastleigh DO.

The Eastleigh office was about half the size of that at Brighton, but Ron reckoned that the 14 staff there could absorb the relatively minor modifications required on the Bulleid locomotives without much upset.

The Ashford DO was the smallest of the three, just eight staff, and was fully engaged on the design of the 1,750 hp diesel-electric locomotive commenced in Southern days. Two examples were to be constructed and a third variant had been authorised for design work to start in the near future.

With Brighton being the largest locomotive drawing office and having the greatest number of experienced staff, Ron arranged that the majority of new steam design would be covered there. He had found a house in Burgess Hill, on the Northern fringe of Brighton and, selling the home in Derby, the family moved down to the South Coast location in the summer of 1950.

Shortly after settling in at the Brighton office, Ron received a request from Riddles to prepare a report on progress of the 'Leader' to date. He speedily got to work and by the 10th March issued his first assessment. This included some comments on the design concept as a whole in the conclusions: 'The design has certain attractive features, it has many problems to solve, and it has some fundamental defects. That the locomotive could be made to work I have no doubt, but a great deal of experimental work will be necessary'.

He had also listed some essential changes to the design in order that the locomotive could be considered serviceable. These were self-aligning bearings, changes to the grossly over-heated fireman's compartment, more development work on the sleeve valves and the employment of smaller wheels.

This report gave Riddles much ammunition in his, by then, obvious desire to cancel the whole programme, but he did permit a further series of tests using a dynamometer car, to prove once and for all, the absolute deficiencies of the design as it stood. Ron was charged with overseeing these tests.

The Chief Civil Engineer having banned the 'Leader' from the Central Section of the Southern Region due to its excessive axle loading, meant that the test programme had to be transferred to Eastleigh on the Western Section. The ban had been enforced by the sudden realisation that the actual axle loading of nearly 25 tons was some 25 per cent in excess of the design value which had been used up to then. Weight control during the design process had clearly not been of great accuracy, probably due to the unorthodox layout involved, coupled to many last-minute and progressive modifications as early testing proceeded.

Bulleid, who had a consultancy agreement with British Railways, resigned from this and was now away in Ireland at Inchicore as their CME, so there was no longer any pressure from him to continue any development.

On 13th April, 1950, the 'Leader' steamed away from Brighton for the last time, being taken as a light engine to Eastleigh where, after adjusting the ballast weights needed to counter-balance the offset boiler, a reweighing was to be carried out. Following a month's layup while the test programme was arranged, a series of trials between Eastleigh and Fratton and, subsequently, Woking and Guildford were made. All appeared to go without a major fault until, on the 29th June, the crank axle of the leading bogie fractured. Following this Riddles could, quite justifiably, have ordered the cessation of all future trials and the withdrawal of the prototype. However, he requested that the the test programme continue with the

Eastern Region dynamometer car and also agreed to the proposal to compare results with a similar series of tests on a Maunsell 'U' class 2-6-0. No. 31618 of that class was originally selected and subsequently replaced by No. 31630.

The test programme proceeded and was eventually completed fairly satisfactorily and the results incorporated in a final report written by Ron for Riddles. The data gave Riddles all he needed to make a strong case to the Railway Executive for the scrapping of this controversial design. The 'Leader' coal and water consumptions were 68 per cent and 48 per cent greater than the 'U' on the same tasks. Bearing in mind that the latter was essentially derived from the 1917 'N' design, this was not a good omen. The Riddles memorandum was issued on 20th November, 1950, just a couple of weeks after a final test run of the condemned locomotive from Eastleigh to Woking with a 480 ton train. This run was faultless, with the engine steaming magnificently and it was almost if it was showing, at the very last, what it might achieve with a bit of further development. However, murmurings were afoot at BR Headquarters about the eventual replacement of steam in the UK, a fact which was to evolve in less than two decades. Riddles had his way, and the 'Leader' disappeared to the scrap lines at Eastleigh, with the remaining four examples, in various states of build, being stored for a short time before being subjected to the cutter's torch.

His position at Brighton ensured that he was on the design committee, chaired by E.S. Cox, which oversaw the BR Standard locomotive design tasks. With him from Brighton he had W. Durban, Mechanical Engineer-Design. To represent the LM Region were C.S. Cocks and J.W. Caldwell, the Western Region supplied F.C. Mattingley and G.E. Scholes, whilst the Eastern and NE Regions supplied E. Windle. Robert Riddles had the overall charge of the policy matters and was the link to the British Transport Commission. In keeping with the plans for giving the individual technical centres specific classes of locomotive to design, certain components which were to be standard parts were given to specific centres for design and detailing. Brighton was allocated the brake and sanding systems for the whole range of standard types.

The new steam designs given to Brighton were two of what eventually turned out to be a range of 12 new standard locomotives built between 1950 and 1960. The BR management, although aware of the inevitability of diesel-electric and all-electric motive power, appeared to place great reliance on steam. It was, after all, well-proven, reliable and sturdy amongst other things and, with Riddles as CME giving backing to its continued development along conventional lines, considerable priority was given to the programme.

On 30th January, 1951 the first of the new British Railways Standard class '7' Pacifics, No. 70000, was to be named *Britannia* in a ceremony at Marylebone Station. The Minister of Transport, the Rt Hon Alfred Barnes MP, was to carry out the naming and many of the elite of BR were to be present. The locomotive had been designed at Derby, with scheming well under way when Ron was moved to Brighton. He had received an invitation to attend this event and, knowing this, Riddles sent a letter inviting him to lunch after the ceremony. What transpired at this luncheon meeting is not on record, but doubtless much of the conversation was concerned with design progress at Brighton, plus a general run through the 'Leader' test results.

A BR class '4' 2-6-4T takes shape at Brighton in October 1951.   *Jarvis Collection*

The first production 2-6-4T No. 80010 stands ready for trials from Brighton.   *Jarvis Collection*

Whilst the 'Leader' tests had been carried out, the larger part of the Brighton drawing office was occupied in the detail designs of the BR Standard 2-6-4T and 4-6-0, both of power classification 4. These had been schemed at Derby to Riddles specifications and it was up to Brighton to take the line diagrams and turn them into products.

The 2-6-4T was, to all intents and purposes, a slightly shortened version of the Fairburn redesign of the Stanier LMS 2-6-4T, itself a taper boiler variant of the Fowler 2-6-4T which had been designed at Derby in the mid-1920s. The Fairburn design was, in fact, still in production at Brighton, where a batch of 41 was being erected as Ron took office, so the switch to the BR design was relatively easy. There were some detail differences with the Fairburn variant, the boiler pressure had been raised from 200 to 225 psi, the cylinder diameter reduced from 19 to 18 inches and the wheel diameter reduced by one inch to 5 ft 8 in. The overall tractive effort was slightly greater at 25,100 lb. compared to the 24,670 lb. of the older design.

No. 80010, the first of the 130 eventually built at Brighton was out-shopped there on the morning of 7th July, 1951 after being weighed. That same afternoon it was fired up and dispatched to Three Bridges and back on its works trials. After final adjustments it went into service on 13th July on largely local turns. On 18th July it was put onto the 11.05 am Brighton to Victoria (via Eridge) passenger service returning on the 3.52 pm Victoria to Brighton on the same route. A log of this last run was taken and, despite time lost taking water at Oxted, this was comfortably made up and arrival at Brighton was 4 minutes ahead of schedule. Shortly afterwards this first production version was allocated to Tunbridge Wells West shed. The class eventually totalled 155, with 15 being built at Derby and 10 at Doncaster. In fact, the last of the class, No. 80154, was the last steam locomotive to be built at Brighton works, in March 1957, for plans were afoot to run down this facility for eventual closure.

In conjunction with the design of the 2-6-4T, the Brighton office had been given the task of designing the class '4' 4-6-0. This was basically a smaller version of the Stanier 'Black Five', which had only ceased production at Horwich in early 1951.

This 4-6-0 was derived for mixed-traffic work and aimed at replacing some obsolescent 4-4-0s then in service, and required as wide a route availability as possible. The boiler was a lengthened version, 9 inches on the front parallel ring, of that fitted to the 2-6-4T, and many other components, cylinders, much of the motion, wheels, bogie and boiler mountings were also common with the tank. Production of this type was to be undertaken at Swindon from 1951, with Brighton works fully committed to the 2-6-4T. Some 80 were to be built in total and were eventually to be found over the Southern, Western and London Midland Regions of BR, more often than not on passenger services such was their capability for fast work.

One experimental programme which had been under way for some time before Ron arrived at Brighton was the testing of a mechanical stoker on 'Merchant Navy' class No. 35005 *Canadian Pacific*. This had been instigated under Bulleid in 1948 but was to be terminated. The cost of incorporating the mechanical stoker, which had to be imported from the USA, was some £1,600 per locomotive. Coal consumption was some 25 per cent above hand firing, due to the smaller coal pieces required for the stoker to function properly. Some calculations based on this increased coal consumption soon made a case for not

R.G. Jarvis

Standard 2-6-4T No. 80010 at Three Bridges on its first trial run from Brighton on 9th July, 1951.

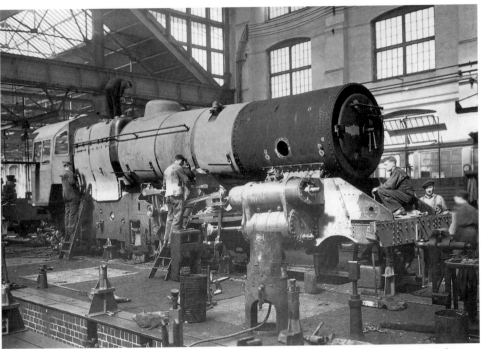

Whilst most of the class '4' tanks were built at Brighton, the class '4' 4-6-0 was a Swindon product. Here No. 75000 is under construction there.   *Jarvis Collection*

The Ivatt influence is very apparent in this portrait of the class '4' 4-6-0.   *Jarvis Collection*

Before too many class '4s' had been turned out the type was put through its paces on the Swindon test plant.

Jarvis Collection

A controlled road test of the class '4' 4-6-0 under way on the former GWR main line near Swindon on 17th January, 1952; engine No. 75006 with a 546 ton train, steam rate 19,000 lb./hr.

Jarvis Collection

proceeding any further. There was also the problem, also found in the early 1930 pulverised coal trials, of the incredibly dirty conditions on the footplate plus the fact that on the train a thick layer of grit found its way through ventilation openings into corridors and compartments, even onto dining tables! In 1951, the locomotive was converted back to its former hand-fired condition.

One little extra duty to come Ron's way in early 1951 was the delivery of a lecture to the Enginemen's Mutual Improvement Class at Stewart's Lane. This lecture covered the design philosophy behind the new Standard locomotives being developed and built for British Railways. With the class '4' 4-6-0 and 2-6-4T being designed at Brighton it made sense for Ron to talk to the Southern Region crews who would soon be handling the new arrivals.

In the railway modelling sphere, Ron found some spare time at Burgess Hill to recommence his hobby, this time concentrating on producing some exquisite hand-made models of bogie coaching stock. He had been involved in this for some time when something caught his attention in North Wales, the rescue of the derelict Festiniog Railway by a group of enthusiasts who had ambitious plans to resurrect this ancient narrow-gauge line. He remembered it of old from those family holidays in that area and kept his eye on the railway press for developments. So began a long association with the Festiniog Railway which was to become an important part of his retirement life.

Rosemary, now approaching her eighth birthday, was sent to the nearby school at Burgess Hill, which Ron and May eventually found rather unsuitable for their daughter. Ron's position at Brighton, coming with a comfortable salary, meant that private education could be budgeted for. She was, in due course, sent to a boarding school, St Brandon's, at Clevedon. This particular school was noted for catering for daughters of the clergy and Ron used to recount the times he received correspondence from the school addressed to the Revd R.G. Jarvis. He mentioned this to his assistant at Brighton and joked that perhaps he should wear his collar back-to-front, being told quite seriously that he would have to do considerably more than that!

'The Lees', the Burgess Hill home of Ron and family whilst the Brighton assignment lasted.
Mrs R. Boorne

One type in use in Wales when the class '9' arrived was the 'Austerity' 2-8-0. Here No. 90201 prepares to haul a lengthy freight on 7th July, 1953.   *R.G. Jarvis*

Austerity 2-8-0 No. 90315 at Builth Road on freight duties, 29th June, 1953.   *R.G. Jarvis*

Chapter Eight

Another BR Standard, the 2-10-0

Amongst the many jobs which were placed at Brighton was the important one of designing new front ends for the Maunsell 'U' and 'N' class 2-6-0s which had been serving the Southern Region so well on mixed-traffic duties. Ron had always regarded the Maunsell 2-cylinder 2-6-0s as the precursors of the BR Standard locomotives and that wheel arrangement was a very useful one for a general purpose medium-sized engine. As they became older there were troubles with the smoke-box bottoms, due to corrosion, requiring the renewal of parts in that area, and the obvious thing to do was to provide a fabricated saddle. At the same time cylinders were wearing out and having to be replaced, so he took the opportunity to have new cylinders designed with improved steam passages and external steam pipes. This was a very similar operation to that carried out on the Fowler 2-6-4Ts which he had in mind from his Derby days (when Stanier, in 1933, was still producing the final batch of Fowler tanks before introducing his own taper boiler version, he introduced a new front end including external steam pipes).

The drawings for this were completed in December 1952 at Brighton and, as the 'N' and 'U' came in for major overhauls they were fitted in the 1955-61 period. But with withdrawal coming from 1962 only 23 of the 'U' and 29 of the 'N' classes were actually modified.

Perhaps the most controversial, yet very successful, of the BR Standard steam locomotives was the 2-10-0 intended for heavy freight work. Starting life as a 2-8-2 layout (shades of the Hughes/Fowler studies of the early 1920s!) it had been intended to use a large number of components from the 'Britannia' 4-6-2, including the boiler, possible with this layout. However, it was felt that a change to the 2-10-0 format would be an advantage, particularly when starting heavy freight trains. On starting the dynamics of a steam locomotive means that a considerable amount of weight is transferred to the rear. In the case of a 2-8-2 this would result in extra weight being transferred to the rear pony truck from the front, thus reducing that available for adhesion. The 2-10-0 layout ensured that this weight transfer was available on the coupled wheels at all times. A sure-footed start was therefore much more likely. Although, it should be said that had the suspension of the trailing truck of the 2-8-2 been compensated with the springing of the rear driving wheels, the reversion to a 2-10-0 may not have been necessarily the outcome. However, amongst British locomotive engineers this feature had never taken serious root, despite the fact that it was fairly common elsewhere, particularly on the Continent.

As with several of the BR Standard designs, the initial layout was schemed at the Development drawing office at Derby. The people involved in this scheme were Eric Langridge and Ron's old colleague of pre-war photographic jaunts, Frank Carrier. So good was the layout produced by these two very experienced designers, that Ron and the Brighton drawing office did not have to make any dimensional alterations to those derived by Langridge and Carrier.

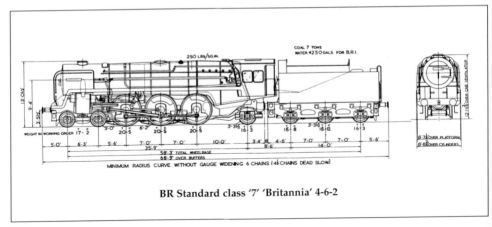

BR Standard class '7' 'Britannia' 4-6-2

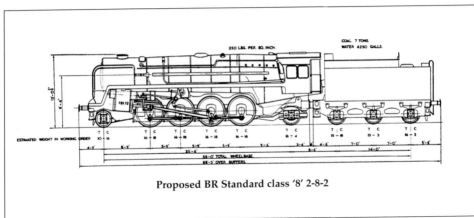

Proposed BR Standard class '8' 2-8-2

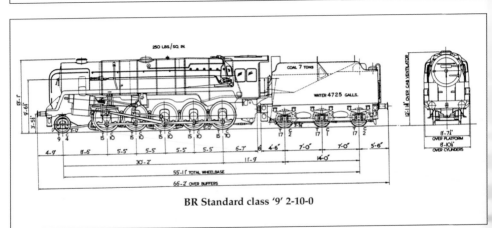

BR Standard class '9' 2-10-0

One disadvantage of switching to the 2-10-0 was that a new boiler had to be designed, the 'Britannia' version not fitting satisfactorily. It was possible to use the class '6' 4-6-2 pressings for boiler plates and the class '7' front tubeplate. A new, shallower, firebox, the back half of the grate being level, was designed. The resulting boiler became the BR type '9' and needed pitching very high to enable the wide firebox to fit over the rear coupled axle. This, as we shall see, was useful when it came to fitting the special boiler designed for the Crosti version. However, the limited space for the deep ash-pan did produce a somewhat awkward feature, in that the pan tended to fill up quickly, placing a limit on the time the locomotive could remain in service before requiring some remedial attention.

The 2-10-0 layout was, to Ron, a perfectly logical wheel arrangement, fully in keeping with his own thoughts, which are borne out by a comment to be found in a letter sent to Stanier from Turkey in September 1941, viz: '. . . when shortly we find it necessary to design a larger freight engine of the 2-10-0 or 4-8-0 type, which would enable us to haul our existing freight trains faster'. In the decade which followed this letter his thinking had not changed and it is interesting to note the 1941 comment on fast running, for the 2-10-0 that resulted, as we shall see, was most certainly capable in that respect.

Despite its long coupled wheelbase of 22 ft, the class '9' was capable of negotiating a six chain curve, this being assisted by having the centre driving wheels flangeless. In order to get the Chief Civil Engineer to grant the route availability desired, the maximum axle loading on the coupled wheels was to be kept to 15 tons 10 cwt. This meant that the hammer blow resulting from the vertical component of the balancing of the reciprocating masses (i.e. piston heads, rods, crossheads and part of connecting rods) needed to kept at a minimum.

A design problem arose in providing the balance weights needed to balance the required percentage of both fore-and-aft forces and the swaying couple,* as had been conventional practice in the UK. Because the substantial big-end of the connecting rods had to clear the very restrictive bottom corners of the BR loading gauge envelope, the lateral position of the rods limited the width of balance weights in the wheel. Spreading the balance weights round too much of the circumference of the relatively small wheel was obviously ineffective.

Fortuitously at that time brother Jim had made a special study of locomotive balancing at the University of Illinois during 1951. He was aware of the satisfactory riding performance of the Bulleid Pacifics, whose three-cylinder arrangement eliminated fore-and-aft inertia disturbance, but nevertheless gave rise to a considerable swaying couple which, however, produced no undesirable effect on their riding characteristics. Accordingly he saw no need to balance the swaying couple on a large two-cylinder locomotive, but only dealt with the fore-and-aft effect. This allowed the balance weights to be smaller, causing lower hammer-blow per wheel, which would be in phase for both wheels on an axle, However, axle and total engine hammer blow would not be reduced. Jim had forwarded this proposal to his chief, not expecting it would merit an application at that stage. Fortunately it found its way to Ron's office, and provided the key for accommodating adequate balance weights.

* The swaying couple is the dynamic force induced by the vertical forces of the reciprocating masses which produces a side to side rocking of the locomotive, which is damped out on the springs.

Jim Jarvis at Roanoke works of the Norfolk & Western Railway, Virginia during his two year scholarship at Illinois University in the USA.   *J.M. Jarvis*

Class '9' No. 92003 on iron ore train from Rogerstone to Ebbw Vale 13th May, 1954. *R.G. Jarvis*

The class '9' locomotives, in later years, were recorded as having achieved very high speeds in passenger service, at least two instances of 90 mph have been recorded with perfectly acceptable riding characteristics.

As regards the frames for the class '9', the design of these was unique in that with the boiler pitched well above them combined with the outside two-cylinder layout, it was possible to provide a considerable number of deep vertical plate stretchers plus a continuous horizontal plate stretcher from the saddle to the ash-pan, this located just above the level of the horn spaces. The whole assembly was extremely torsionally stiff and made a solid foundation for the remainder of the locomotive's structure.

Although it only had a very brief life-span, the class '9' most certainly acquired a reputation for reliability and ease of servicing. It was also popular with enginemen, representing the very latest in design features intended to give them every assistance in operating the locomotive. Ron's meticulous approach to the layout of the cab details on this, and the previous class '4' designs, was responsible for this. Robert Riddles was heard to observe that a great deal of credit for the success of this engine must go to Ron Jarvis as the engineer responsible for the production of the detail drawings at Brighton. Also, Col H.C.B. Rogers, the railway biographer and historian, quoted in his book on the 2-10-0: 'There are some grounds for regarding it as the most outstanding steam locomotive ever to run in this country'.

The design task for the class '9' fell conveniently between the two class '4' locomotives and the Bulleid Pacific rebuilds. The Brighton team accomplished the task of detailing the engine for production by the middle of 1953 and an initial order for 20 was placed on Crewe works. There were some interesting variations on the basic design, the first of which was the production of a batch of 10 fitted with a Franco-Crosti boiler.

The story goes that E.S. Cox, Riddles' right-hand man for design matters at HQ, spent a holiday in Italy during which he paid a visit to the running sheds near Venice of the Italian State Railways. Here he came across several locomotives fitted with the Fanco-Crosti boiler (*see Appendix Two for a description of this feature*) and, having been given a footplate ride, had been introduced to Dottore Ingeghere Piero Crosti, the inventor. Impressed by the enthusiasm of Dr Crosti, Cox returned to the UK determined to try out this type of boiler which appeared to offer substantial fuel savings. He asked Ron Jarvis to take on the responsibility of visiting the Continent to assess the performance of locomotives employing the Crosti boiler, so in June 1951 Ron departed to West Germany to look into some recent applications on the Deutsche Bundesbahn, his destination being Minden.

Ron was greeted at Minden by Dr Ing Muller, responsible for locomotive testing and research, Dr Ing Schorning, district motive power superintendent, Dr Crosti himself and Wing Commander Roper Robinson of Messrs Franco-Crosti.

Based at Minden were two class '52' war locomotives 'Kriegsloks', of which several thousand had been constructed during the war. The two examples modified with the Crosti boilers were, in fact, built in January 1951 by Henschel in order to use up some of the partly finished components to hand. Their numbers were 52.9000 and 52.9001.

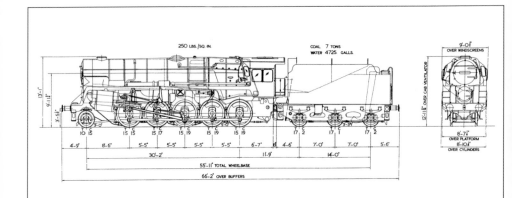

BR Standard Crosti class '9' 2-10-0

The Crosti boiler batch of class '9s' was built at Crewe in 1955. Here a boiler assembly approaches the chassis.   *Jarvis Collection*

Following an initial meeting with the officials Ron embarked on a footplate run on No. 52.9000 in normal freight service between Minden and Seelze with a 1,400 ton load, during which the locomotive appeared to be very easy to fire and was never short of steam. The cut-off was 30 per cent, except for starting, and the normal boiler pressure of 240 lb./sq. in. was easily sustained. It was noticeable that the pull on the fire was very even, presumably due to the long gas circuit. Dr Muller stated that a coal saving of between 6 per cent to 14 per cent was obtained when compared to a standard class '52' which had a Henschel feed-water heater and was already very efficient.

Upon his return to England Ron wrote up an account of his visit and findings and submitted this to BR Headquarters. The response was speedy, for a batch of ten 2-10-0s was ordered to be fitted with Franco-Crosti boilers, BR having come to an agreement as to how the Societa Per Azioni Locomotive a Vapore Franco-Crosti were to be recompensed for their design.

The Brighton drawing office team set to work on this interesting task, and immediately found that the layout of two pre-heaters, as on the German locomotives, had to be modified to a single, central, pre-heater unit. This was caused by the restrictions of the British loading gauge. Ron had no option but to order that a new boiler unit be designed, it not being possible to mount the existing unit over a centrally located pre-heater drum. The class '9' boiler was already at the highest pitch permissible.

Despite the difficulties caused by loading gauge restrictions, the final scheme was arrived at quite speedily and the final locomotive, viewed from the left side, looked perfectly normal. Only when viewed from the right side was the unorthodox layout apparent in the shape of the asymmetrically-disposed exhaust chimney wrapped around the boiler just in front of the firebox. The new boiler had a reduced heating surface of 1,432 sq. ft as against the 2,015 sq. ft of the standard boiler, the super-heater areas were also affected, 411 sq. ft compared to 535 sq. ft for new and standard respectively.

The Crosti-boilered modification was tested thoroughly at the Rugby test plant and compared with a standard '9F'. Apart from the rather unlucky event of the standard locomotive. No. 92050, being a particularly good example (in that its coal and water consumption had always been noted as being lower than the average for the class), the economies found with the Crosti version were much lower than those anticipated. The maximum saving of fuel consumption was just 8.35 per cent, a far cry from the 20 per cent anticipated. This value was insufficiently large enough to justify any payment to the designer. There were also considerable troubles with corrosion in the chimney passages caused by sulphurous deposits from the low exhaust temperatures of the Crosti system. The 10 locomotives which incorporated this feature entered traffic but were never popular with the crews as the exhaust fumes, from the chimney located in front of the firebox, not only obscured the lookout on the right-hand side, but were prone to being drawn onto the footplate and filling the cab. Eventually, by 1962, the 10 locomotives had the pre-heater assembly removed and finished their lives with the smaller boiler as normal types, but tended to be short of steam if driven hard.

The end result viewed from this side shows the unorthodox location of the exhaust chimney.

Jarvis Collection

The opposite looks remarkably conventional as seen in this photograph of the first example, No. 92020 at Crewe, 20th April, 1955.

Jarvis Collection

A Crosti 2-10-0 under way. This was taken from Ron's office window at Brighton, 9th
September, 1955.   *R.G. Jarvis*

2-10-0 No. 92023, one of the Crosti batch, on test at Rugby in 1955.   *Jarvis Collection*

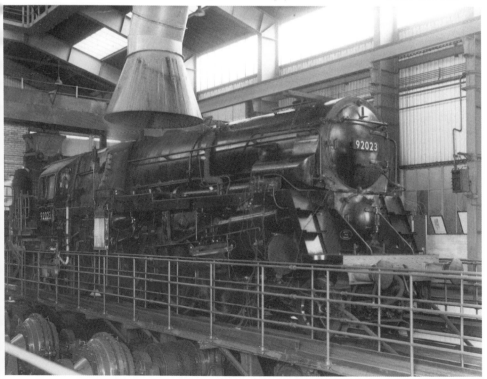

Early batches of locomotives had a problem with the regulator in that, due to some springiness in the operating mechanism, at high values of cut-off the steam pressure prevented the valve from shutting completely, thus causing uncontrolled slipping when starting away. A batch of the first 20 had been placed at Ebbw Junction motive power department for working the iron ore trains up Ebbw Vale. Ron visited South Wales to talk to the motive power department representatives and engine crews regarding this problem, which it appears could be overcome, in the short term, by adjustment of the regulator mechanism to minimise the excessive springiness. The root cause appeared to be that the demand for steam from the cylinders was such that this outstripped the supply flowing through a partly-opened regulator valve. The boiler pressure therefore became much higher than that in the steam pipes and clamped the partially opened valve so tightly that the driver was unable to move it through the rather springy mechanism. The cure that Ron produced was deceptively simple, the smaller regulator valve used on the class '4' 4-6-0 was fitted. This produced a local restriction in the steam circuit but this never seemed to produce any ill-effects in service. The smaller surface area produced a lower clamping force, which could be overcome by the regulator linkages from the cab.

The crews were otherwise very pleased with the '9F', finding it powerful and free-running and capable of hauling trains of up to 600 tons unaided up the steep grades. Even with cut-offs of 60-70 per cent the boiler pressure was maintained within a few pounds of 250 lb./sq. in. all the time.

With such positive feedback on the '9F' it is easy to understand why the design was kept in production in a time of planning for the end of steam. The ruggedness and reliability of this 2-10-0 made it a popular type, whilst its free-running characteristics were such that it was frequently found on passenger services. For a locomotive with 5 ft driving wheels this was a remarkable achievement and vindicated the new approach to balancing.

North-West Wales was still a popular destination for the Jarvis family and it was during these that evidence of the restoration of the narrow-gauge Festiniog Railway (FR) became evident. Ron and his brother Jim became interested in keeping up with this ambitious programme of the enthusiasts who were determined to rebuild this railway. In 1957 the brothers Jarvis made a point of travelling to Portmadoc in order to attend the AGM of the fledgling organisation and began to follow events in some detail. Ron rapidly became interested in the restoration programme taking shape on the FR. Whilst his technical expertise was associated with locomotive design and operation, he had a deep seated interest in railway carriages. He could see involvement in the FR carriage and wagon department as fulfilling this interest in a practical way. The railway, in 1954, had a stock of some 20 carriages, all in a deplorable condition. Some were worse than others and none had been in use since 1939 when the passenger service ceased.

A number had been stored under cover, the best of which could be fairly rapidly made usable to enable a service to be started. Gradually, the other carriages were repaired and brought into traffic until all that remained were a small number of vehicles which appeared to be practically hopeless to repair, most certainly uneconomic by normal standards.

One bright spot was the discovery of a reasonably repairable vehicle of the same gauge in a field near Barnstaple in Devon. This was a relic from the Lynton & Barnstaple Railway, closed in 1935 by the then owner the Southern Railway. Once he had learnt of the existence of this carriage, Ron began to campaign for it to be acquired for the FR. His insistence won and the railway purchased that vehicle in 1959, had it dismantled on site and the components transported to the Boston Lodge works at Portmadoc. It was subsequently modified and rebuilt to produce a magnificent buffet car, in the process of which it became the pattern for a number of new carriages which were built in future years for the FR.

Amongst the stock were two antique carriages, Nos. 15 and 16. These two vehicles had been built in 1872 and it is certain that they were the first bogie carriages to run in the UK. The Midland Railway had been the first to introduce bogie carriages on the standard gauge in 1874, these were of a Pullman design imported as sub-assemblies from the USA. In addition to the bogie vehicles were three little four-wheeled coaches which were to become Ron's responsibility after launching out on No. 16. Bogie No. 15, although in bad condition, was repairable and dealt with first by the FR, whilst Ron could turn his attention to No. 16. This latter coach had spent 15 years out-of-doors at the Harbour station, Portmadoc, exposed to the elements. Much of the panelling and timber framing was rotted through and needed complete renewal. In fact, the list of replacement parts soon spread to the mouldings, roofing, flooring and refurnishing - in other words, a complete new body assembly was called for. Once examination of the vehicle had taken all this in, some proposed that it was only fit for burning, being totally beyond repair. They reckoned without Ron's determination, however, and he offered to undertake the rebuild of the framing single-handed, using his workshop at Burgess Hill. And so began what was to be a lengthy exercise, with visits to North Wales in the caravan to take measurements and make patterns for a complete new framing structure for No. 16.

The limited time available for this restoration exercise was further reduced by the heavy workload at Brighton and later, at Derby. However, the move to Derby in 1965 did bring Ron nearer his goal, in terms of driving distance, and matters progressed more speedily thereafter. The model railway work, which had, up to then, occupied the workshop space, was put on one side and the larger scale took its place.

With Bank Holidays and part of his annual leave calling for frequent visits to the Boston Lodge Works of the Festiniog Railway, Ron bought a caravan which he and May towed to Wales to use as a base on the longer visits.

Meantime, whilst the FR restoration task was germinating there was much to occupy Ron at Brighton. The 2-10-0 was proving a versatile and popular locomotive and, although the decision to end steam in the mid-1960s had been made, was in production up to 1960. In all 251 were built, the largest number of any BR Standard design. In fact, out of the total numbers of all Standard classes of 999, some 486 were Brighton designs. Nearly 50 per cent!

Only two further modifications were tried out on the class '9'. The first being a batch of three, Nos. 92165-7, which were built with mechanical stokers. Notably these had double chimneys to assist in the draughting for combustion of the mechanically fed small coal. As with the earlier 'Merchant Navy' mechanical stoker trials, the fuel consumption was increased considerably and

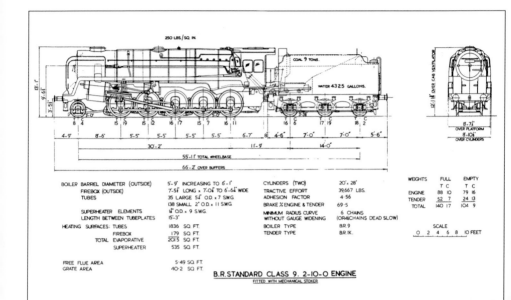

BOILER BARREL DIAMETER (OUTSIDE)	5'-9" INCREASING TO 6'-1"	CYLINDERS (TWO)	20' x 28"		WEIGHTS	FULL	EMPTY
FIREBOX (OUTSIDE)	7-5½" LONG x 7-0½" TO 6-6½" WIDE	TRACTIVE EFFORT	39,667 LBS.			T C	T C
TUBES	35 LARGE 5⅛" O.D. x 7 SWG.	ADHESION FACTOR	4·56		ENGINE	88 10	79 16
	138 SMALL 2" O.D. x 11 SWG.	BRAKE % ENGINE & TENDER	69·5		TENDER	52 7	24 13
SUPERHEATER ELEMENTS	1⅛" O.D. x 9 SWG.	MINIMUM RADIUS CURVE	6 CHAINS		TOTAL	140 17	104 9
LENGTH BETWEEN TUBEPLATES	15'-3"	WITHOUT GAUGE WIDENING	(OR 4 CHAINS DEAD SLOW)				
HEATING SURFACES: TUBES	1836 SQ. FT.	BOILER TYPE	B.R.9			SCALE	
FIREBOX	179 SQ. FT.	TENDER TYPE	B.R.1K.		0 2 4 6 8 10 FEET		
TOTAL EVAPORATIVE	2015 SQ. FT.						
SUPERHEATER	535 SQ. FT.						
FREE FLUE AREA	5·49 SQ. FT.						
GRATE AREA	40·2 SQ. FT.						

B.R. STANDARD CLASS 9. 2-10-0 ENGINE
FITTED WITH MECHANICAL STOKER

Left: A batch of three 2-10-0s were fitted with the Berkeley mechanical stoker. This shows the equipment as fitted.   *Jarvis Collection*
Right: The mechanical stoker drive unit to be fitted. Into the tender of a 2-10-0.   *Jarvis Collection*

The sole example of the BR Standard class '8' Pacific which entered traffic. No. 71000 *Duke of Gloucester*, is now preserved.   *Jarvis Collection*

the experiment did not proceed any further. The double chimney, however, was applied to many of the later batches of 2-10-0s.

The second modification was the fitting of a Giesl ejector and oblong chimney to ascertain if any economies were forthcoming. Ron had, in December 1960, visited Austria to investigate the results of this particular feature on the locomotives of the Austrian Federal Railways. On this trip he met the inventor of the apparatus, Dr A. Giesl-Gieslingen.

Accordingly, No. 92250, the final 2-10-0 to be built at Crewe, was fitted with a Giesl ejector and chimney and, in 1961, was sent to Rugby for a comprehensive series of tests. As with the Crosti boiler, little was gained by this modification and, with the imminence of the end of steam, it was deemed uneconomic to modify any further examples. About the only positive feature was the capability to achieve adequate performance using poor quality coal, which the Austrian Federal Railways were constrained to do. The UK supplies were still of reasonable quality and, indeed, were soon to be eclipsed as a means of providing heat energy for the railways as they switched to the more modern prime movers.

There was also one underlying fact which had a determining affect on all experiments to do with using low-grade fuel in the UK, this being that, no matter what the calorific value of the coal, the NCB charged BR the same price. Had a more realistic pricing policy been based on the heat content we might well have seen wider adoption of mechanical stokers, Crosti boilers and Giesl ejectors applied as steam ended its days.

However, there was one small compensation in respect of the unmodified Bulleid Light Pacifics still in service. One particular feature of the Giesl-fitted locomotives was the big reduction in spark-throwing obtained. This was a current problem on the un-rebuilt Bulleid Light Pacifics with frequent complaints coming in from farmers about damage to crops from passing trains. Ron had, on his return from Austria, proposed that the 50 remaining unmodified locomotives should be fitted with Giesl ejectors and chimneys. Authority was obtained for a trial on one example and No. 34064 *Fighter Command* was so fitted at Eastleigh in 1962. Apart from reducing the spark-throwing dramatically, this modification considerably improved the steaming such that the locomotive's performance was judged to be equal to a 'Merchant Navy'. However, with steam's days numbered no further members of that class were modified.

One final trial on a 2-10-0 was this one of a Giesl ejector. Dr Giesl became a good personal friend of Ron Jarvis and is pictured here in front of the test locomotive at the Rugby test station.

Jarvis Collection

Chapter Nine

The Bulleid Pacific Rebuilds

Eastleigh had been the office where the 'Merchant Navy' class was designed and, although the 'West Country' class was designed at Waterloo, until the staff had been bombed out of there, and subsequently at Brighton, the Bulleid Pacific drawings were held at Eastleigh.

By March 1950, when Ron took over the Brighton office all the 30 'Merchant Navy' locomotives were completed and in service and the last batch of five 'West Country' engines were under construction in the three Southern Region works. Erection of the latter had, for the most part, been at Brighton with one batch at Eastleigh.

As Ron himself wrote:

> The Bulleid Pacifics were undoubtedly remarkable locomotives. The basic concept of a three-cylinder 4-6-2 with 6 ft 2 in. diameter wheels and a really first-class boiler was excellent. The frame incorporated good principles, although it suffered from detail defects, and the cylinders were well located. As vehicles the locomotives were very good, providing excellent riding characteristics.

The strong point of both classes was the boiler, which steamed excellently, making it capable of producing high power outputs for sustained periods. In the 1948 interchange trials the Bulleid Pacifics had shown this time and again, at the expense of high specific fuel consumption. However, locomotives are provided to haul trains and not achieve a figure of so many (or rather so few) pounds of coal per drawbar horse-power hour, as Ron succinctly put in a paper.

In 1950, the availability of these Pacifics was, to put it mildly, appalling. Some 40 per cent of the 'Merchant Navy' class were out of service at shops or sheds, together with 29 per cent of the 'West Country' class. Against the normal figure for non-availability of 10-15 per cent, this was unacceptable. Once settled in office Ron, amongst the many other responsibilities, began to assess the Pacific situation and quickly compiled a list of features requiring attention. These were:

1. Inadequate stiffness of the front frame which flexed considerably, causing fractures of the bogie centre support, steam and exhaust pipes in the smoke-box and frame fractures themselves.
2. Immense problems with the valve gear, involving wear of all pins and corrosion of parts in the oil bath. The 3:8 levers driving the piston valves wore heavily, so heavily that two out of three were scrapped at each overhaul. Considerable over-run of the piston valves occurred due to the motion brackets working loose. The oil bath lost oil in large amounts due to the pumping action of the motion and the sump often fractured and oil leaked onto the track, much to the annoyance of the Civil Engineer. [In fact, in Ron's correspondence the following comment came to light: 'With the Gresley gear only one of the cylinders was liable to have an inferior steam distribution, whereas with the Bulleid it applied to all three'.]
3. The air-smoothed casings caused fires which occurred frequently (38 cases in 1953) due to oil mist covering the underside of the boiler getting mixed with dust to form a highly flammable substance.

The new centre cylinder for the 'Merchant Navy' rebuild. Note the substantial frame stretcher attached to the front. The top of both assemblies forms the smokebox saddle.   *Jarvis Collection*

The first rebuild, No. 35018 *British India Line*, nears completion at Eastleigh.   *Jarvis Collection*

4. The smokebox had a flat top which pulsated under the effects of the exhaust vacuum, the resulting movement being severe enough to loosen chimney bolts.
5. Both the cast steel and fabricated pony trucks were prone to fractures.
6. The 'West Country' had drop grates and fire-bars which sagged and jammed the operating mechanism.
7. Intermediate drawbar failures occurred, luckily never at high speed - the prospect of an engine separating from its tender was always a possibility.
8. The drive to the mechanical lubricator was flimsy.
9. The steam reversing gear suffered from frequent pipe failures and tended to wander. (In fact on one occasion, when Ron was taking a footplate ride on No. 34071 *601 Squadron* on the 'Golden Arrow', it wandered into full reverse at 75 mph when the driver tried to notch up slightly!) [As a matter of interest, this same problem of going into reverse is still with the unmodified locomotives, as the driver of No. 34072 *257 Squadron* confirmed to the writer in October 2002 at Swanage, but at a more manageable 20 mph!]
10. All but the last 10 of the 'West Country' locomotives were not fitted with ash-pan dampers, making the fire difficult to control at times.
11. Difficulties were experienced in filling the tenders with water from some existing columns, the rave at the rear being too high.

From the above list, some modifications were occupying much of the Eastleigh office. But these were only of an intermediate nature and it seemed logical, once authority had been granted for a complete rebuild, to incorporate all the remedies needed to eliminate the problems leading to non-availability.

Before this authority could be given, some grounds for the costs involved needed assessing against the clearly large increase in maintenance costs caused by the frequent stoppages.

Some of the minor modifications indicated by Ron's survey could be initiated quite speedily and the Eastleigh drawing office was ordered to scheme drawings for some six items. These were:

1. Stiffening of the front frames
2. Strengthening of the 3:8 levers and bearings
3. Replacing the unsatisfactory cylinder and steam-chest drain-cocks
4. Welding on additional webs to the pony truck frame
5. Strengthening the mechanical lubricator drive
6. Minor tender changes - cut away raves and provision of tunnels for the fire irons

Authority was given to modify three each of the 'Merchant Navy' and 'West Country' classes, the engines concerned being labelled the 'Guinea Pigs'. These minor changes improved matters somewhat and were subsequently made to other locomotives as they passed through the shops for repairs.

Whilst the above was under way and the final major modifications for the complete rebuild were being considered, a problem with bent coupling rods arose on the 'Merchant Navy'. This was becoming very frequent and was causing a considerable loss of availability. Eventually, when it was discovered that these bent rods were being straightened *in situ* at the sheds by means of a hydraulic jack, off a convenient wall, something had to be done. E.S. Cox, learning of this procedure and the number of times it was being applied, sent an instruction to Ron to design new rods which would not become permanently

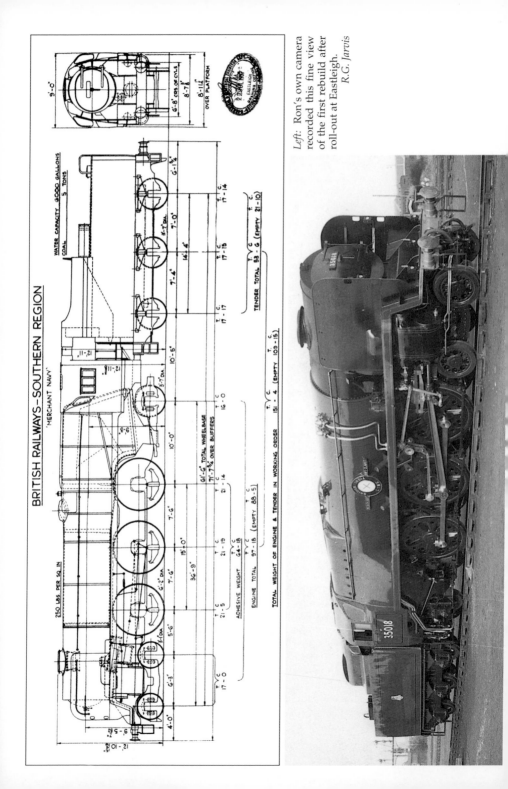

Left: Ron's own camera recorded this fine view of the first rebuild after roll-out at Eastleigh.
R.G. Jarvis

bent. These were to be designed without delay and fitted to all 'Merchant Navy' locomotives.

Ron dug back into his archives, finding notes on a theory based on the principle of a coupling rod being able to absorb as much energy as possible during the condition most likely to cause bending, e.g. slipping of the driving wheels. This strain energy theory had been introduced to him back in his early days at the LMS Derby Research Department, by a young research engineer, S.R.M. Porter, who had died in 1935 at the age of just 27. Using these notes, Ron designed rods of rectangular section high strength steel, sufficiently flexible to bow outwards and thus absorb the energy caused by the dynamics of the slipping. These new rods produced a complete solution to the problem. In fact their strength was tested to the extreme when an axle-box failed on a West of England express at Farnborough, the coupling rod not being pulled apart by the repeated bending this caused until the train reached Gillingham in Dorset, some 71 miles further on.

A short time later there was a failure of a crank axle at speed, near Wincanton. The locomotive was not derailed other than the one wheel of the fractured crank axle. The root cause of the failure was the high stresses due to the imbalance resulting from having unbalanced crank sweeps. Ron initiated some urgent calculations on the stressing of the crank axle which showed that the stresses were well above the fatigue limit at the speeds involved (80 mph). The analysis also showed that, for the Bulleid Pacifics, the fatigue life was likely to be short and that most of the 'Merchant Navy' examples, at their current mileages, could be categorised as imminent failures. All the class were immediately withdrawn from service for modification with redesigned crank axles.

By this time it was obvious that the full rebuild was going to require modified crank axles to permit three independent sets of valve gear to be used. The sprocket for the original chain-driven valve gear was therefore spigotted to the right-hand crank sweep and its balance arm, which had been added to eliminate the imbalance causing the high stresses. This arrangement was also capable of taking the eccentric for the new valve gear when the rebuild programme was initiated. This also made the crank axles interchangeable between modified and unmodified locomotives.

With 30 'Merchant Navies' out of service, the shortfall in express motive power was catered for by the transfer of ex-LNER 'V2s' and ex-LMS 'Black Fives'. The Western Region at its Swindon works provided much of the manufacturing capacity for the new crank axles.

Other modifications for the rebuild programme varied from the simple to the complex. On the 'West Country' class the situation regarding the crank axles was not so desperate, as they had not been in service as long as the 'Merchant Navies' and they were dealt with as they passed through the shops, or as ultrasonic testing indicated the start of a fatigue crack.

One particular feature of all the Bulleid Pacifics was the relatively high boiler pressure of 280 lb./sq. in. At starting steam had to be throttled to prevent slipping, whilst at speed due to over-running of the valves on the original designs the best means of control was the regulator. Also, even at short cut-offs, full regulator produced very high powers. The free-steaming of the boilers

No 35005 *Canadian Pacific* at Rugby shed on 1st March, 1950, fitted with a mechanical stoker for tests on the line.   *J.M. Jarvis*

No. 35022 *Holland America Line* in unmodified guise is here to be found on the Rugby test plant, 8th April, 1953.   *J.M. Jarvis*

meant that the additional energy available was seldom, if ever, used. Accordingly, it was decided to restrict the boiler pressure to 250 lb./sq. in. The reduction of 30 lb./sq. in. should not be missed, it was felt.

Some suggestions were ignored, for example, in the early days of the investigative work the suggestion came from BR Headquarters that a rebuild to a two-cylinder layout might well be required. Ron took careful note to put this on one side as it would result in such major changes to the locomotive as to destroy the existing design concept, which in principle was sound enough.

There remained a further batch of major modifications required to complete the ultimate rebuild, viz :

1. The switch to three independent sets of valve gear
2. A new centre cylinder and front frame stiffening
3. A new smokebox assembly
4. Deletion of the air-smoothed casing

The Brighton office was, at that time fully committed on the support of the BR Standard class '4' 2-6-4T and 4-6-0, plus the design of the 2-10-0 and the 2-10-0 with the Crosti boiler, when the order to proceed on the Pacific came through from Mr A. Smeddle, the deputy Regional CM&EE. Ron accordingly set up a small development section under Michael Lockhart to achieve the redesign, which was, by now, an extremely urgent task.

The basic remit to which Ron was constrained to work is probably best put in his own words from a letter to Col H.C.B. Rogers in later years: 'The whole principle of the exercise was to eliminate the unsatisfactory features and retain the many excellent ones the original design included. Moreover, nothing was to be changed unless there was a very clear case for making a change.'

The first big problem was to see if three sets of Walschaerts valve gear could be applied, if possible, to the existing cylinders. It was soon evident to Ron that the middle cylinder would have to be replaced and the steam-chest moved to one side to line up with the valve gear in the space between the connecting rod and the right-hand frame plate. One feature of the new inside cylinder assembly was that the valve had inside admission as against the previous outside admission. This eased the worries about access for maintenance of the glands which would only be exposed to exhaust pressure. The outside cylinder valve glands were easily accessible for any rectification needed. The resulting middle engine drew heavily on those employed on the 'Schools' class and the Stanier 'Jubilee'.

The outside cylinder valves were located such that it was possible to link onto the new valve gear, the original units could therefore be used.

The manufacture of a new inside cylinder assembly enabled a new fabricated smokebox saddle to be provided, which was bolted to the front of the cylinder casting. The whole assembly made a very solid bracing for the front frames.

The new outside Walschaerts gear was very similar to that on the BR class '4' 2-6-4T. A modification had to be made to the final drive to the valve spindle based on the need to translate the actuation to the cylinder vertical centre line. Here Ron's knowledge of some German valve gears, picked up in Turkey all those years ago, came in useful to guide the draughtsman detailed to cover this change.

No. 35025 *Brocklebank Line* on the Swindon test plant. Note the old GWR dynamometer car behind.

So, having dispensed with the Bulleid valve gear and lubrication by means of an oil bath, it only remained to fit a new manual reversing gear, remove the air-smoothed casing and fabricate a new cylindrical smoke-box plus a large number of relatively minor changes to complete a sorely needed redesign. Design work went ahead and, once the details had been completed the financial authority for the expenditure needed to convert the classes was required. Ron drew up a report from his findings and submitted this to BR Headquarters as evidence for the need to spend the money. *Appendix Three* gives some of the arguments put forward in this report, which resulted in authority for 90 locomotives, 30 'Merchant Navy' and 60 'West Country' to be converted.

The resulting designs improved the locomotives so far as the reliability and availability were concerned and, for the final years of steam on the Southern Region, they reigned supreme as the best of the express motive power on that line. Although some decried the rebuilt engines as an insult to their designer, as Ron himself expressed a final comment concerning them in the closing paragraph of his classic paper covering the rebuild: 'And the locomotives themselves: at least 90 per cent of each was still Mr Bulleid's engine'.

The 50 unmodified locomotives, all 'West Countries', stayed in service as the end of steam approached. They had been fully maintained to the normal schedule along with the modified locomotives, so were in good condition throughout. Withdrawal took place as heavy repairs became necessary after a certain date before the end of steam.

A contrast in size and design. 'Terrier' No. 32650, originally LBSCR No. 50 of 1876 (now preserved) sits beside 'West Country' rebuild No. 34003 *Plymouth*.   *Jarvis Collection*

One little task Ron took upon himself was to alter the lining-out as specified by diagrams issued
by the Railway Executive prepared at Derby. Although the diagrams suited LMS locomotives
they were not ideal for classes of other railways. This shows the original on an ex-SR class 'L'.
J.M. Jarvis

The much simpler and more suitable lining-out specified by Ron.   *J.M. Jarvis*

Chapter Ten

The Steam Transition Period at Brighton

By the end of the 1950s and the implementation of the Modernisation Plan for BR it was clear that the days of the steam locomotive were numbered. A change to other forms of motive power was beginning to accelerate. With the Southern Region having a large proportion of its tracks electrified it was only the West of England services that were the domain of steam. In the East more electrification was taking place and diesel units taking over cross-country routes as yet to be electrified. The only regular services requiring steam were the still fairly extensive boat train services to the Kent Channel ports and, of course, the 'Schools' 4-4-0s still covered the Hastings line. Even these last two were, in the 1960s, to succumb to electric and diesel units respectively.

The class '9' 2-10-0 represented the climax of steam locomotive production for BR and the rebuilt 'Merchant Navy' and 'West Country' numbers stayed at 30 and 60 respectively for the final dying years of steam on the Southern Region. In 1958 it was obvious that locomotive manufacture at Brighton was at an end, just repair work filled the shops. It had proved impossible to extend the works due to its hillside location and the proximity of the main line into Brighton station. Modernisation was therefore not possible, and with the imminent demise of steam, facilities geared to the maintenance and construction of that form of motive power were not to be required in the future. By the end of 1958 even repair work was phased out and gradual closure began. By 1960, when the last 2-10-0 had emerged from Swindon and the last 'West Country' rebuilds were emerging from Eastleigh, the emphasis at the Brighton drawing office was transferred to diesel, diesel-electric, electric and electro-diesel locomotive developments.

With the Crosti-boilered class '9' in service and appearing to operate satisfactorily, the Brighton team were asked to look at the possibility of using a Crosti-type boiler on the BR Standard class '5' 4-6-0s fitted with Caprotti valve gear, of which some 20 were in service. A scheme had been prepared by Crosti showing how this might be done and Ron and his staff prepared a feasible design. However, with the end of steam just a few years away, this project got no further than the drawing board. It was, in fact, quite probably the last steam project to appear from any of the Regional design centres.

With his trips to Germany in connection with the Crosti boiler investigations, Ron had formed a close relationship with Adolf Dormann, who was the Deutches Bundesbahn (DB) motive power superintendent, Mainz Division, based in Frankfurt. This friendship deepened to a point where they met with their wives on social occasions. Some years later, Ron was on a visit to Germany with the Institution of Locomotive Engineers. One of the visits they made was to the Mainz Division which was still under Dormann's control. The party was travelling in a special train provided by the DB and, upon their departure from there Ron, at the insistence of Dormann, was on the footplate of the locomotive. This could not fail to be noticed by members of the party, some of whom were from the top brass of BR, and caused some raising of eyebrows.

Several diesel exercises had been well under way when Ron took over at Brighton, revolving mainly around a batch of 25 0-6-0 diesel-electric shunters built in 1949 and a single diesel-mechanical prototype No. 11001 provided by Messrs Davey, Paxman & Co. for comparative tests on the Southern Region. The diesel-electrics were based largely on the successful 1937 designs of Maunsell, of which three had been provided before war intervened to cease production. In addition there were the Ashford, designed diesel-electrics, of which the first two were put into service in 1951.

The saga of diesel shunter No. 11001 dragged on for many months and the locomotive was plagued with minor, but annoying, faults. The 600 hp engine was satisfactory but the gearbox proved troublesome, although some of this was thought to be due to inadequate oil changes in the box. It was a six-coupled design with a jackshaft drive and the cab was placed at the gearbox end. The weight prepared for service was 49 tons. It was placed in service at Norwood where trials continued for some months, and comparative data obtained with this single example and a standard 0-6-0 diesel-electric and two steam locomotives, a Maunsell 'Z' class 0-8-0T and an old Billinton 'E4' class 0-6-2T.

The Norwood trials at an end, a meeting was organised at Brighton on 6th July, 1951. One clear conclusion was that No. 11001 certainly showed clear advantages over the steam locomotives in terms of fuel cost and immediate availability, but the capital cost of £19,436 was high. Due to the somewhat erratic reliability it was decided that this type was unsatisfactory for other examples to be purchased and it was dispatched to the Eastern Region in the Leeds area in July 1952, where it spent much time under repair at Derby works interspersed with sporadic work at Leeds. Returning to the Southern Region in 1956, it ended its days at Redhill. It was withdrawn in 1957, having run just 46,818 miles since coming into traffic. The equivalent diesel-electrics had, in the same time, clocked up over 259,000 miles each.

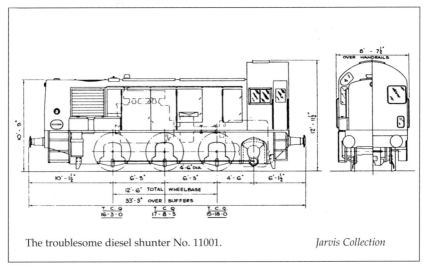

The troublesome diesel shunter No. 11001.   *Jarvis Collection*

The Brighton works shunter No. 377s hauls the thoroughly modern ex-LMS diesel-electric No. 10001 during a visit for servicing and comparison with the SR example.
R.G. Jarvis Collection

So far as diesel developments were concerned, 1954 was a noted for a special event at Brighton, as at one time that year all five larger diesel-electric main-line locomotives then operated by BR were at the works. Nos. 10000 and 10001, the LMR variants, were, at that time, allocated to the Southern Region to concentrate all five for operation and maintenance. The three SR variants, Nos. 10201-3, the first two of 1,750 hp and the third of 2,000 hp were also in residence. There had been some evidence of wheel tyres working loose after heavy braking on all five locomotives and some investigations were under way to determine the optimum interference fit for shrinkage of the tyre onto the wheel. For moving the diesels around the works the resident shunter was called into service, It seemed rather bizarre to see these large modern locomotives being shunted around by the Stroudley 'Terrier' No. DS377, later BR No. 32635 but, as so often happened, Ron had his camera to hand, as witness the illustration above.

By the time the British Railways Modernisation Plan had been drawn up, the emphasis on extending electrification over more of the Regions was increasing. Some 25 per cent of all passenger train mileage of BR was already electrically operated, much of this on the Southern Region. On this Region it was realised that whilst much of the existing routes would be covered by multiple-unit trains there were some services which would benefit by the employment of electric locomotives. These were those covering the Continental services, both passenger and freight, via Folkestone and Dover. It was determined that an electric locomotive of some 2,500 hp output of the Bo-Bo layout and weighing some 80 tons should suffice. A meeting was held at Brighton on 25th August, 1955 to discuss the general specification and outline. Design of the mechanical parts of the locomotive was to be carried out at Brighton.

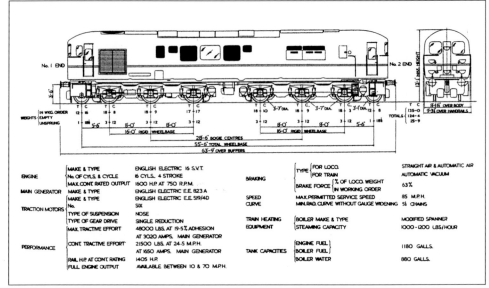

ENGINE	MAKE & TYPE	ENGLISH ELECTRIC 16 S.V.T.	BRAKING	TYPE	FOR LOCO.	STRAIGHT AIR & AUTOMATIC AIR
	No. OF CYLS. & CYCLE	16 CYLS., 4 STROKE			FOR TRAIN	AUTOMATIC VACUUM
	MAX.CONT RATED OUTPUT	1600 H.P. AT 750 R.P.M.		BRAKE FORCE	% OF LOCO. WEIGHT IN WORKING ORDER	63%
MAIN GENERATOR	MAKE & TYPE	ENGLISH ELECTRIC E.E. 823 A	SPEED	MAX. PERMITTED SERVICE SPEED		85 M.P.H.
TRACTION MOTORS	MAKE & TYPE	ENGLISH ELECTRIC E.E. 519/4D	CURVE	MIN.RAD.CURVE WITHOUT GAUGE WIDENING		51 CHAINS
	No.	SIX				
	TYPE OF SUSPENSION	NOSE	TRAIN HEATING	BOILER MAKE & TYPE		MODIFIED SPANNER
	TYPE OF GEAR DRIVE	SINGLE REDUCTION	EQUIPMENT	STEAMING CAPACITY		1000 -1200 LBS/HOUR
PERFORMANCE	MAX. TRACTIVE EFFORT	48000 LBS. AT 19.5% ADHESION AT 3020 AMPS. MAIN GENERATOR		ENGINE FUEL		1180 GALLS.
	CONT. TRACTIVE EFFORT	21500 LBS. AT 24.5 M.P.H. AT 1650 AMPS. MAIN GENERATOR	TANK CAPACITIES	BOILER FUEL		
	RAIL H.P. AT CONT RATING	1405 H.P.		BOILER WATER		880 GALLS.
	FULL ENGINE OUTPUT	AVAILABLE BETWEEN 10 & 70 M.P.H.				

Plan of 1,600 hp type '3' 1C-C1 diesel-electric locomotives Nos. 10201 and 10202. No. 10203 was rated at 1,750 hp.   *Jarvis Collection*

The third SR diesel-electric, No. 10203, completed under Ron Jarvis in his early days at Brighton. Seen here on a test train at Salisbury, 28th June, 1955.   *R.G. Jarvis Collection*

Diesel-electric No. 10001 on the 4.15 pm Euston-Bletchley service passing South Kenton, 16th May, 1959.   *R.S. Carpenter Collection*

A feature of all SR electric locomotives, when utilising third-rail current pick-up was the need to cater for 'gapping', or running over sections of track such that the collector shoes were not in contact with the third rail at level crossings or complex point networks. Some means of providing a current supply was needed and supplied by a 'booster' set comprising of a motor-generator set driving a heavy flywheel which would, for a limited time, be capable of providing current to the traction motors. This principle had been proven in the earlier Co-Co electric locomotives designed and built under Bulleid which had employed two motor-generator sets. However, the reliability of that equipment was such that one set should suffice, thus saving cost and weight for the projected design.

By June 1956, the design task was well under way and the selection of the type of bogie design was under review from a number of schemes prepared by Ron's team. Later that year a regular series of meetings were commenced between the SR Electrical Engineer's Office at London Bridge, the English Electric Co., suppliers of motors and electrical equipment, and the Brighton drawing office. Following Ron's suggestion, based on his earlier visits there, the Swiss Locomotive and Machine Works were contacted as advisors in the field of motor drive arrangements. The SLM had extensive experience on the design and employment of electric locomotives for some decades and their expertise was much valued. In fact, the co-operation was extended to cover the axle-boxes and guides, which were to be of SLM design.

The initial order for a batch of thirteen 2,500 hp locomotives was placed on the Doncaster locomotive works with delivery of the first example to be by mid-1958. Construction proceeded and No. E5000 was out-shopped a few months late in December 1958. When they entered service, the 'E5000' class were the most powerful single units running on British Railways. This was

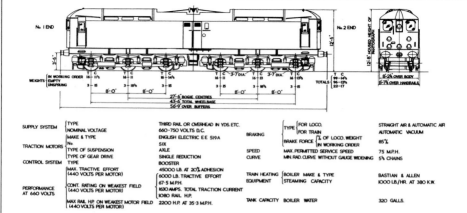

SUPPLY SYSTEM

TYPE	THIRD RAIL OR OVERHEAD IN YDS. ETC.
NOMINAL VOLTAGE	660-750 VOLTS D.C.
MAKE & TYPE	ENGLISH ELECTRIC E E 519A

TRACTION MOTORS

No.	SIX
TYPE OF SUSPENSION	AXLE
TYPE OF GEAR DRIVE	SINGLE REDUCTION

CONTROL SYSTEM

TYPE	BOOSTER

PERFORMANCE AT 660 VOLTS

MAX. TRACTIVE EFFORT (440 VOLTS PER MOTOR)	45000 LB. AT 20% ADHESION / 6000 LB. TRACTIVE EFFORT / 67·5 M.P.H.
CONT. RATING ON WEAKEST FIELD (440 VOLTS PER MOTOR)	1630 AMPS. TOTAL TRACTION CURRENT / 1080 RAIL H.P.
MAX RAIL H.P. ON WEAKEST MOTOR FIELD (440 VOLTS PER MOTOR)	2200 H.P. AT 35·3 M.P.H.

BRAKING — TYPE { FOR LOCO. / FOR TRAIN }	STRAIGHT AIR & AUTOMATIC AIR / AUTOMATIC VACUUM
BRAKE FORCE % OF LOCO. WEIGHT IN WORKING ORDER	85%
SPEED — MAX. PERMITTED SERVICE SPEED	75 M.P.H.
CURVE — MIN. RAD. CURVE WITHOUT GAUGE WIDENING	5¼ CHAINS
TRAIN HEATING EQUIPMENT — BOILER MAKE & TYPE / STEAMING CAPACITY	BASTIAN & ALLEN / 1000 LB./HR. AT 380 K.W.
TANK CAPACITY BOILER WATER	320 GALLS.

The first Southern electric locomotive designed under Bulleid before Nationalisation.

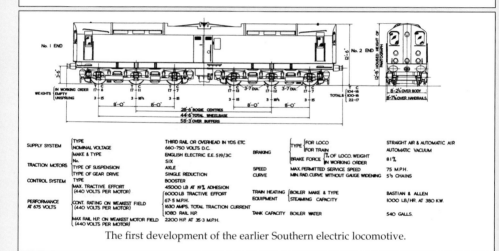

SUPPLY SYSTEM

TYPE	THIRD RAIL OR OVERHEAD IN YDS ETC
NOMINAL VOLTAGE	660-750 VOLTS D.C.
MAKE & TYPE	ENGLISH ELECTRIC E.E. 519/3C

TRACTION MOTORS

No.	SIX
TYPE OF SUSPENSION	AXLE
TYPE OF GEAR DRIVE	SINGLE REDUCTION

CONTROL SYSTEM

TYPE	BOOSTER

PERFORMANCE AT 675 VOLTS

MAX. TRACTIVE EFFORT (440 VOLTS PER MOTOR)	45000 LB. AT 19% ADHESION / 6000 LB. TRACTIVE EFFORT / 67·5 M.P.H.
CONT. RATING ON WEAKEST FIELD (440 VOLTS PER MOTOR)	1630 AMPS. TOTAL TRACTION CURRENT / 1080 RAIL H.P.
MAX RAIL H.P. ON WEAKEST MOTOR FIELD (440 VOLTS PER MOTOR)	2200 H.P. AT 35·3 M.P.H.

BRAKING — TYPE { FOR LOCO / FOR TRAIN }	STRAIGHT AIR & AUTOMATIC AIR / AUTOMATIC VACUUM
BRAKE FORCE % OF LOCO. WEIGHT IN WORKING ORDER	81%
SPEED — MAX. PERMITTED SERVICE SPEED	75 M.P.H.
CURVE — MIN. RAD. CURVE WITHOUT GAUGE WIDENING	5½ CHAINS
TRAIN HEATING EQUIPMENT — BOILER MAKE & TYPE / STEAMING CAPACITY	BASTIAN & ALLEN / 1000 LB. AT 380 K.W.
TANK CAPACITY BOILER WATER	540 GALLS.

The first development of the earlier Southern electric locomotive.

SUPPLY SYSTEM

TYPE	THIRD RAIL OR OVERHEAD IN YDS. ETC.
NOMINAL VOLTAGE	660-750 VOLTS D.C.
MAKE & TYPE	ENGLISH ELECTRIC E.E.532

TRACTION MOTORS

No.	FOUR
TYPE OF SUSPENSION	FULLY SUSPENDED
TYPE OF GEAR DRIVE	SINGLE REDUCTION

CONTROL SYSTEM

TYPE	BOOSTER

PERFORMANCE AT 675 VOLTS

MAX. TRACTIVE EFFORT (675 VOLTS PER MOTOR)	43000 LB. AT 25% ADHESION / 12400 LB. TRACTIVE EFFORT / 69·6 M.P.H.
CONT. RATING ON WEAKEST FIELD (675 VOLTS PER MOTOR)	3000 AMPS. TOTAL TRACTION CURRENT / 2300 RAIL H.P.
MAX. RAIL. H.P. ON WEAKEST MOTOR FIELD (675 VOLTS PER MOTOR)	3000 H.P. AT 59·3 M.P.H.

BRAKING — TYPE { FOR LOCO / FOR TRAIN }	STRAIGHT AIR & AUTOMATIC AIR / AUTOMATIC AIR & AIR CONTROLLED VACUUM
BRAKE FORCE % OF LOCO. WEIGHT IN WORKING ORDER	88%
SPEED — MAX. PERMITTED SERVICE SPEED	90 M.P.H.
CURVE — MIN. RAD. CURVE WITHOUT GAUGE WIDENING	4 CHAINS
TRAIN HEATING EQUIPMENT — ELECTRIC HEATING CONT. OUTPUT	300 K.W. AT 675 VOLTS

The E5000 (later class '71') electric locomotive.

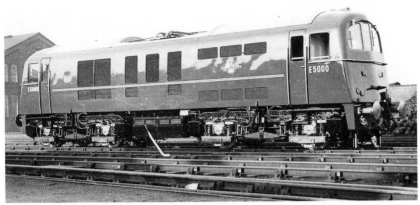

The first of the E5000 series of electric locomotives for the Southern Region appeared from Doncaster Works in 1958.   *R.G. Jarvis Collection*

due to the way in which the drawbar horsepower rose sharply with speed to a maximum of some 3,800 at 48 mph where the switch to weak field was made with a corresponding sharp fall off as speed increased. Even then, there was still 2,000 hp available at 75 mph. A total of 24 were eventually built, a number of which were eventually rebuilt into large electro-diesels. Neither version had a particularly good reputation and were withdrawn relatively early.

With Brighton works a near empty shell it was clear that the days of the design department there were numbered, yet work still kept being placed there, such was the competence and reliability of the team. The final design to emerge under Ron's leadership was the electro-diesel of 1,600/600 hp capacity, the former rating in pure electric locomotive concept, the latter as a diesel-electric. The 2,500 hp electric locomotives being restricted to the electrified lines, something was needed to cater for the lines over which electrification was yet to appear. Currently these were mainly steam, but the withdrawal deadlines were approaching fast and replacement motive power would be needed. Also the ability to be used in the diesel-electric mode for shunting operations was a distinct advantage as few of the yards on the Southern Region had been fitted with overhead cables for current collection. In fact it was this particular feature which lead to the requirement for an electric locomotive capable of being worked away from the power supply.

By deliberately restricting the diesel power to 600 hp, using the same power-plant as that employed in some existing dmu sets then in service, permitted the design to be priced below that of an equivalent diesel-electric of some 1,600 hp. 600 hp was also very adequate for all shunting operations likely to be encountered plus being adequate for continued traction, at reduced speeds, of sizeable trains, both passenger and freight, should the current supply to the third rail be cut off at any time. Also this locomotive could be coupled to a set

An official photograph of the Vulcan Foundry-built electro-diesel locomotive No. E6007.

Jarvis Collection

The 1,600/600 hp electro-diesel locomotive (later class '73').   *Jarvis Collection*

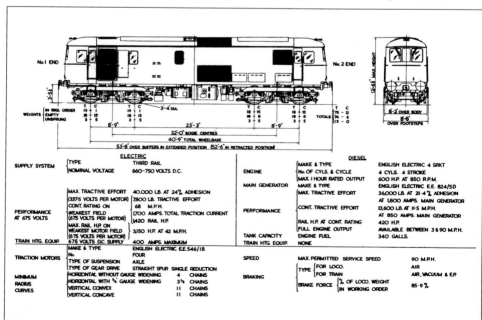

	ELECTRIC			DIESEL	
SUPPLY SYSTEM	TYPE	THIRD RAIL	MAKE & TYPE		ENGLISH ELECTRIC 4 SRKT
	NOMINAL VOLTAGE	660-750 VOLTS D.C.	ENGINE	No. OF CYLS. & CYCLE	4 CYLS. 4 STROKE
				MAX. I HOUR RATED OUTPUT	600 H.P. AT 850 R.P.M.
			MAIN GENERATOR	MAKE & TYPE	ENGLISH ELECTRIC E.E. 824/5D
	MAX. TRACTIVE EFFORT	40,000 LB. AT 24% ADHESION		MAX. TRACTIVE EFFORT	36,000 LB. AT 21·4 % ADHESION
	(337·5 VOLTS PER MOTOR)	7800 LB. TRACTIVE EFFORT			AT 1,800 AMPS. MAIN GENERATOR
	CONT. RATING ON	68 M.P.H.		CONT. TRACTIVE EFFORT	13,600 LB. AT 11·5 M.P.H.
PERFORMANCE	WEAKEST FIELD	1,700 AMPS. TOTAL TRACTION CURRENT	PERFORMANCE		AT 850 AMPS. MAIN GENERATOR
AT 675 VOLTS	(675 VOLTS PER MOTOR)	1,420 RAIL H.P.		RAIL H.P. AT CONT. RATING	420 H.P.
	MAX. RAIL H.P. ON	3,150 H.P. AT 42 M.P.H.		FULL ENGINE OUTPUT	AVAILABLE BETWEEN 3 & 90 M.P.H.
	WEAKEST MOTOR FIELD		TANK CAPACITY	ENGINE FUEL	340 GALLS.
	(675 VOLTS PER MOTOR)		TRAIN HTG. EQUIP.	NONE	
TRAIN HTG. EQUIP.	675 VOLTS D.C. SUPPLY	400 AMPS. MAXIMUM			
	MAKE & TYPE	ENGLISH ELECTRIC E.E.546/1B			
TRACTION MOTORS	No.	FOUR	SPEED	MAX. PERMITTED SERVICE SPEED	90 M.P.H.
	TYPE OF SUSPENSION	AXLE		TYPE {FOR LOCO.	AIR
	TYPE OF GEAR DRIVE	STRAIGHT SPUR SINGLE REDUCTION		{FOR TRAIN	AIR, VACUUM & E.P.
MINIMUM	HORIZONTAL WITHOUT GAUGE WIDENING	4 CHAINS	BRAKING		
RADIUS	HORIZONTAL WITH ¾ GAUGE WIDENING	3½ CHAINS		BRAKE FORCE {% OF LOCO. WEIGHT	85·9 %
CURVES	VERTICAL CONVEX	11 CHAINS		{IN WORKING ORDER	
	VERTICAL CONCAVE	11 CHAINS			

of coaches with a driving trailer and used in a push-pull capacity, further increasing its flexibility.

Some careful thinking was going to be needed to accomplish this design so Ron was overjoyed at the initial order for six prototypes for thorough testing before series production. So many previous designs had gone into service before the bugs had been ironed out, resulting in failures and costly modifications. There was to be a front end mock-up which was examined in detail by representatives from the Operating and Motive Power Departments. Suggestions were made and acted upon where practicable. Even a representation was made of the end of a coach which could be set to represent any track curve to enable all hoses to be coupled up to ensure there was no fouling. Another mock-up covered part of the equipment compartment which was becoming rather cluttered, to ensure that fitters could get past equipment to service the control cubicle and obtain access to brake pipes.

The care with which all this was carried out ensured that, when in production, the minimum of subsequent modifications were needed.

Eastleigh works produced the six prototypes and, following nearly two years of trials, orders for a further 43 were placed, of which 30, Nos. E6007 to 6036, were built by the Vulcan Foundry during 1964-5. One of Ron's last tasks for the Southern Region was to organise a series of meetings at the Vulcan Foundry works to oversee the commencement of production of that batch.

Whilst all the electro-diesel work was going on, in 1959 a requirement for a number of diesel-powered shunting locomotives for Southampton Docks was put out by the British Transport Commission. Some two dozen proposals were tendered, out of which two were short-listed, both from Ruston & Hornsby. Technical matters were to be dealt with by the Brighton Office and Ron was quickly drawn into the discussions taking place. It was arranged that the Southern Region send representatives to a meeting at Messrs Ruston & Hornsby at which their range of diesel-hydraulic and diesel-electric locomotives suitable for the Southampton requirement be investigated. Ron took with him H.S. Smyth, one of his key people. Interestingly, one of the two BTC representatives was Ron's brother, Jim, who came with H.L. Butler. To round off the party, Southampton Docks sent Messrs A.B. Rashleigh and A.S. Larkin.

Several locomotives were inspected, with performance details being furnished and, following assessment a recommendation was made that an order for 14 diesel-electric locomotives be placed on Ruston & Hornsby. With a wheelbase of 8 ft 7 in. the 0-6-0 shunters were capable of negotiating curves of 2 chains which abounded in the complex trackwork on the Docks system. Their maximum tractive effort was 28,240 lb., adequate for moving heavy freight traffic around. The specification was agreed in April 1961 and delivery set for 1962.

The selection of the Ruston & Hornsby diesel-electric was probably influenced by an earlier assessment of some nine different makes of 0-6-0 shunting locomotives. This had been put into a report issued in early 1958 following the consideration of a range of diesel-electric, diesel-mechanical and diesel-hydraulic types ranging from 190 hp to 225 hp in power. Although none of those listed in that report were selected at the time, the general findings were biased towards the Ruston & Hornsby submission.

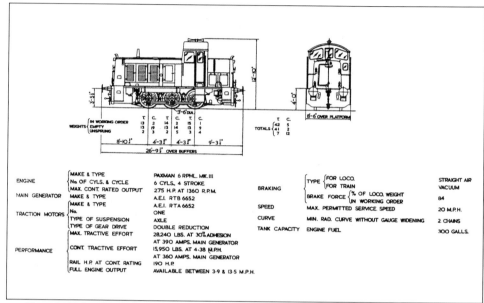

ENGINE	MAKE & TYPE	PAXMAN 6 RPHL. MK.III
	No. OF CYLS. & CYCLE	6 CYLS. 4 STROKE.
	MAX. CONT. RATED OUTPUT	275 H.P. AT 1360 R.P.M.
MAIN GENERATOR	MAKE & TYPE	A.E.I. RTB 6652
TRACTION MOTORS	MAKE & TYPE	A.E.I. RTA 6652
	No.	ONE
	TYPE OF SUSPENSION	AXLE
	TYPE OF GEAR DRIVE	DOUBLE REDUCTION
	MAX. TRACTIVE EFFORT	28,240 LBS. AT 30% ADHESION AT 390 AMPS. MAIN GENERATOR
PERFORMANCE	CONT. TRACTIVE EFFORT	15,950 LBS. AT 4-38 M.P.H. AT 360 AMPS. MAIN GENERATOR
	RAIL H.P. AT CONT. RATING	190 H.P.
	FULL ENGINE OUTPUT	AVAILABLE BETWEEN 3-9 & 13-5 M.P.H.

BRAKING	TYPE FOR LOCO.	STRAIGHT AIR
	FOR TRAIN	VACUUM
	BRAKE FORCE % OF LOCO. WEIGHT IN WORKING ORDER	84
SPEED	MAX. PERMITTED SERVICE SPEED	20 M.P.H.
CURVE	MIN. RAD. CURVE WITHOUT GAUGE WIDENING	2 CHAINS
TANK CAPACITY	ENGINE FUEL	300 GALLS.

Plan of 275 hp diesel-electric shunter (later class '07'). These Ruston & Hornsby locomotives were used in Southampton Docks.   *Jarvis Collection*

An official photograph of Ruston & Hornsby 275 hp diesel shunter No. D2986.

Jarvis Collection

Chapter Eleven

The Return to Derby and the HST

Early in 1963, changes were about to take place on the upper strata of BR management. General Sir Brian Robertson was retiring as Chairman and his place was being taken by Dr Richard Beeching. A complete restructuring of the top levels of management was organised after this change took place, with much more coming under the direct control of the BR Board by the deletion of a layer of management at Regional level. The various Regional drawing offices then came under HQ control.

By the early 1960s it was clear that the Brighton office's days were coming to a close and Ron received a promotion to the post of Mechanical Engineer (Design) in the BR Board's Chief Mechanical Engineer's Department at Eastleigh. Initially, this did not mean that he transferred to Eastleigh, the most modern of the three Southern Region works, being able to continue his work from Brighton for the time being. The salary was £2,650, quite a generous sum in those days.

This new position, effective from January 1963, also gave him responsibilities of overseeing the emu side of Southern Region affairs. The two years that followed were, in his own opinion, quite the most rewarding of his whole career. With the carriage and wagon drawing office of the Southern Region, based at Eastleigh, now under his control, the design of new emus for the Bournemouth electrification extension plus other stock to replace the ageing Brighton units, there was plenty to take place of the fast dwindling bustle of Brighton works. In addition plans were being made to provide a use for some of the electro-diesel locomotives on propelling coaching stock over both electrified and other lines.

The workshop at the Burgess Hill home was now in use for the Festiniog bogie coach restoration exercise. Many weekends and Bank Holidays were taken up by visits to Portmadoc with the caravan, often taking coach body parts prepared at Burgess Hill using timber and other materials scrounged from many sources. Sometimes the journeys were affected by adverse weather, like on one occasion, nearing the end of their long drive, they were caught in a very heavy downpour and only just negotiated a deeply flooded section of road before the rapidly rising water reached running board level.

In January 1965, Ron found himself being moved back to his old stamping ground at Derby as Mechanical Engineer, Design, Derby, where he replaced J.W. Caldwell who had retired at the end of 1964. This position put him in charge of both the locomotive and carriage and wagon drawing offices there.

The LDO was still in the London Road building to which it had been relocated in August 1931. It was a typical DO with large windows on three walls, a high beamed ceiling, and each board or desk had its own suspended light. With the wheel having gone full circle over almost three decades the main difference was that Ron now had overall charge of this and the carriage and wagon design office, compared to his earlier days as a very junior draughtsman.

558 Kedlestone Road, Derby, Ron and May's home after Brighton. The caravan used for the forays to Wales is parked outside.   *J.M. Jarvis*

The Derby locomotive drawing office as it was when Ron returned to take charge of it and the carriage and wagon DO in 1964. At the far end can be seen the Nielson valve motion model used to develop valve gear arrangements.   *CM&EE, BRBHQ, Courtesy of J.B. Radford*

Derby, at that time, was busy turning out diesel-electric locomotives, mainly 0-6-0 shunters, 1,160 hp (later 1,250 hp) Bo-Bo and 2,300 hp (later 2,500 hp) 1Co-Co1 main line types and was fast approaching a total of 1,000 diesels produced. The last steam locomotive, BR class '5' No. 73154, had been out-shopped as far back as 1957, bringing to 2,941 the total of steam locomotives built at Derby. The occasional steam type still appeared for repairs with the last example being 2-10-0 No. 92012 in early 1964. Within two or three years steam was no more on BR.

One little project under way as Ron started his new responsibility at Derby was the proposal to modify a pair of standard BR 350 hp 0-6-0 diesel-electric shunters for working in tandem, as master and slave, at a closely controlled low speed.

The office allocated to Ron was in Nelson Street and from here he began his time back at Derby. The initial tasks revolved around the production of the diesel-electrics, plus involvement in the Railcar Committee which he chaired. On this latter assignment his previous experience with the three-car set in 1938-39 was invaluable, for the modern railcar sets, which had been introduced in the mid-1950s, were similar in concept to that pioneering attempt on which the war had intervened to stop progress.

The Burgess Hill home was sold and the family moved up to Derby, to No. 558 Kedleston Road, Allestree, on the northern outskirts of Derby. Here they settled and Ron immersed his spare time in continuing the restoration work for the Festiniog. The journey to Portmadoc was, at least, shorter giving more time in North Wales. About this time Ron and May decided to look for a second home in that area and began searching for something suitable. Although the caravan had been adequate for their frequent visits, they decided that something more permanent would be of benefit. After some searching in the

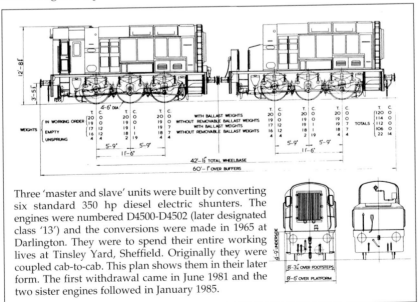

Three 'master and slave' units were built by converting six standard 350 hp diesel electric shunters. The engines were numbered D4500-D4502 (later designated class '13') and the conversions were made in 1965 at Darlington. They were to spend their entire working lives at Tinsley Yard, Sheffield. Originally they were coupled cab-to-cab. This plan shows them in their later form. The first withdrawal came in June 1981 and the two sister engines followed in January 1985.

The last day in the old LDO, Friday 11th March, 1967, before the move to the new technical centre. In the front row, from the left are: K.W. (Ken) Everett, Motion; R.W. Brocklebank, who still lived at Crewe and travelled to Derby each day; S.V. (Stanley) Sykes, Boilers; S.W. (Sid) Holbrook, recently recalled from retirement for his expertise; H.H. (Horty) Owen, assistant chief draughtsman; C.E. (Chris) Peake, chief draughtsman. *CM&EE, BRBHQ, Courtesy of J.B. Radford*

In 1968, Ron achieved 40 years railway service and was presented with this clock as a token of appreciation by the BR Board. *Jarvis Collection*

Portmadoc area, convenient for the FR, they came across a pair of cottages 'Bodawen Lodge' which lay between Portmadoc and Tremadoc. Half this property, which had seen better days, had sitting tenants who remained whilst the remainder was largely derelict.

Both cottages were restored and modernised, the task taking some years. The one to be used by Ron and May was much improved by an entrance hall incorporating doors and panelling rescued from ex-Brighton line Pullman cars. The furnishings also included Pullman car armchairs from the same source. A new staircase was also installed.

These cottages were set in a picturesque part of the countryside and with one half reserved for Ron, May and the family, the other half was still occupied by the sitting tenants.

Although, in the early days, the trips to Tremadoc involved much house and railway restoration work, Ron was happy to use his free time attending to such matters. In this context he was his own boss and could pace his efforts as he felt able, knowing that the end result would be due to all his own efforts. His engineering expertise was often called for on the Festiniog Railway and he was happy to offer advice on many matters. Some years previously, the FR had been in need of funds and raised a fair amount by disposing of the remains of the single Fairlie locomotive built in 1869 and tried out on that line in the early years of steam traction. Ron was saddened by this sale of an historic locomotive, but in later years was to be mainly responsible for persuading the FR to purchase *Blanche* and *Linda* from the Penrhyn Quarries when that organisation closed down their railway operation. With some rebuilding these two locomotives were the mainstay of the FR operations over many years.

The choice of Derby as the design centre for BR was probably in part due to the fact that a comprehensive Research Centre had been established there in the early 1930s, the foundation of which had been laid by Sir Henry Fowler in his final years on the LMS. Research and design together on the same site made sense, as the two disciplines were closely linked.

With his Welsh holiday home sorted and firmly settled back at Derby, Ron was soon to find himself becoming involved in yet another reshuffle by BR top management. A new Railway Technical Centre (RTC) was to be created in 1967, located in a building being constructed between London Road and the southbound main line from Derby station. Much of the staff from the various Regional drawing offices were to be concentrated at the RTC, together with those from the Testing, Inspection and Research Departments plus, for a time, the Workshop Division's HQ staff.

So far as the locomotive drawing office staff were concerned, there were several new faces, to Derby, appearing. From Brighton, via Swindon, came J.G. 'Jimmy' Jones, who had been chief draughtsman at Brighton. Two more ex-Southern people were Wilfred Durban and Stanley Gordon Smith, the former previously Mechanical Engineer, Design at Brighton/Eastleigh and the latter Chief Technical Assistant, carriage and wagons, Eastleigh.

Swindon had its input in A.C.L. 'Arthur' Sly, who had served his apprenticeship and worked in the locomotive drawing office there. He had been much involved in the design of the BR Standard locomotives allocated to

Swindon plus having been closely connected with the design of the diesel-hydraulic locomotives. His favourite quotation was: 'In the ultimate, people are more important than projects', a philosophy which appears to have all but disappeared from the management scenario nowadays.

There were also staff from Wolverton, Doncaster, Darlington and the BRB offices in London to round off the team. Many of these had their own ideas as to how things should be done, and perhaps the hardest thing for Ron to tackle was the moulding of all these different philosophies into a common theme to deal with new designs. Stanier had been in much the same position when he began as CME, but had judiciously imposed his line of thinking by suitable cross-posting of key personnel he knew would listen to him. Conversely, they knew that he would listen to them on crucial matters and, in some circumstances, be willing to adjust his thinking. Ron had hoped to be appointed Director of Design in this big reorganisation. It was, after all, the next step up from his current position in charge of the locomotive, carriage and wagon design. The BR Board had their own agenda, however, and appointed the Assistant Chief Electrical Engineer, Walter Jowett, to the Director of Design post. He had come into the railway sphere from English Electric having been promised the Chief Electrical Engineer post when that incumbent retired. In the event the CME took over the Electrical Department to become CM&EE and Jowett had to be content with his subservient position. It was as though the BR HQ had a penchant for putting noses out of joint!

The position given to Ron in this reshuffle was that of Design Engineer, Locomotives, where he retained control of just the locomotive drawing office. The main activity to be encompassed over the next few years was the design of the power cars for the prototype High Speed Train planned for introduction in the mid-1970s. Ron saw his new responsibilities as a rather 'sideways' move and, with outside interests to attract his expertise, began thinking about finding an opportunity for retirement. The rationalisation and reorganisation taking place on BR was becoming too predominant for his liking. Many key people were beginning to disappear from the scene and, to make matters worse, the budget for new developments was strictly controlled and, in his opinion, inadequate.

His new position produced some challenging opportunities for the mechanical design of locomotives, diesel and electric. The task was to cover the design of the vehicle consisting of structure and running gear, the installation of the power equipment and the arrangement of the whole locomotive. He had a colleague with the title 'Power Equipment Engineer' who was responsible for specifying and selecting the power equipment, braking gear and electrical equipment.

When the reorganisation took place, Ron took advantage of the situation by setting up a new Locomotive Development Section which was charged with the investigation into project design studies for future locomotives. These were assessed in conjunction with the Power Equipment Engineer's section which comprised a group of specialist engineers dealing with the specification of traction and auxiliary power purposes.

With a general reorganisation going on, the large amounts of obsolete data needed dealing with. Ron approached the Director of Design, Jowett, for a ruling on what should be done with the drawings, tracings and other records which, for Derby, went back to the Kirtley/Johnson days. Some decision was needed to enable these to be sorted and properly disposed of. The reply was terse and blunt: 'Oh well, keep about a dozen or so of the most interesting drawings and scrap the rest!'

Without more ado, Ron contacted the Curator of Historic Relics at the Clapham Museum, John Scholes, and came up with a plan to save considerably more than Jowett had indicated. This was to select for preservation all the key engineering arrangement drawings, plus those of all standard components such as boilers, boiler fittings such as injectors, ejectors, plus wheels, motion and axles, etc. He managed to gather together a team from his staff who were willing to work outside normal hours to locate and list the relevant drawings and tracings from the many thousands stored in fireproof cabinets. This took several weeks of work with those to be saved rolled up and a massive pile of less important detail drawings for scrapping.

To add to the above archives, a similar exercise was carried out on the thousands of glass negatives which filled the chief photographer's store-room, dating back to the 1880s. Those selected for preservation were carefully packed into specially made plywood boxes with screw-down lids for sending to Clapham.

Ron also arranged that all the drawings done for the BR Standard locomotives were transferred to Trent House, where they stayed intact until being transferred to the NRM at York, as were the drawings and negatives sent to Clapham. Other archives from Derby, namely the records of works orders, registers of locomotives, diagram books, etc. were also collected together and, in January 1968, transferred to the British Transport Archivist in London. These are now to be found at the National Archives, Kew.

Railway historians and preservation organisations have much to thank Ron Jarvis for in his foresight and stubborn persistence which ensured that so much archive material was rescued from almost certain obliteration.

The chest containing the historic drawings from other sites, which Ron had arranged to be collected together and stored in Ivatt's office in the late 1940s, was still extant and he had this moved into his own office for safe-keeping. In later years, after he had retired, these were all micro-filmed and the originals, in the chest, sent to the NRM where they continue to be a source of valuable information to authors and researchers.

In 1967, during the arrangements under way for the selection and transfer of drawings, tracings, photographic records and other historic data to Clapham, the possibility of preserving one of the two pioneering diesel-electric locomotives, Nos. 10000 and 10001, was raised. Ron asked Brian Radford to produce a report on the condition of these units which then languished in sidings at Derby works and Willesden MPD respectively. They had been withdrawn for some time and had several parts missing, but it was thought possible to recreate one unit for preservation out of the two.

Unfortunately, the Clapham Museum was very pressed for space and, although the locomotive was recognised as valuable in the interests of the National Collection, the proposal was not taken up and both units were eventually scrapped. The diesel-electric advance with the National Collection is

The pioneering diesel-electric No. 10000 sits withdrawn outside Derby works in the 1960s. To the left can be seen the ex-Southern diesel-electric No. 10102, also withdrawn.

R.S. Carpenter Collection

The Midland Pullman 6-car set, which ran for a short time between St Pancras and Manchester, was in many ways a predecessor to the HST.   *Jarvis Collection*

now represented by a much later design, the 'Deltic' prototype, and not one of the unique Ivatt-inspired designs of 1947.

Amongst the normal DO work was a fair proportion of project design work on advanced electric and diesel-electric locomotives which were intended to be produced in quantity in the mid-1970s to meet the assumed needs of BR in the future. Ron, always keen to be in a position to see such developments materialise, was of the opinion that these, if they had been developed, would have placed BR at the forefront of modern locomotive technology. However, the authority to proceed never materialised.

Just one, smaller, electric type, the 100 mph class '87', germinated from this project work, but by the time it entered production and service on the newly completed electrification of the West Coast Main Line between Glasgow and London in 1974, Ron had retired.

There was one glimmer of hope on the horizon, this being the advent of the High Speed Train project. Now that running of trains at speeds up to 100 mph was becoming commonplace and, with the increasing competition from the airlines, the case for a frequent high-speed train service became paramount. One key time for a journey seemed to be three hours, for if a train journey took longer than this, the airlines invariably won. It appeared that a speed of 125 mph could offer a good alternative to the aircraft over distances of up to 350-400 miles. This, of course, was accompanied by the requirement of braking distances being no greater than the existing trains running at 100 mph and it was estimated that, using modern braking technology, a train running at 125 mph was capable of being halted within the limits set by the then current colour-light signal spacing. Keeping the axle loading to the required low level was a major challenge.

A very high power to weight ratio was required to achieve the speeds and accelerations desired and train lengths of no more that nine vehicles, including the power cars, would result from this. As more frequent services were foreseen, shorter train lengths were not thought to present a disadvantage in terms of passenger capacity. Although, once in service, the train length was varied, the class '253' (WR) started off at 2 + 7 being later extended to 2 + 8. The class '254' (ER) on the other hand was 2 + 8 from the start.

Ron's responsibility on this major development, bringing BR up-to-date in railway technology, was the design of the power cars for the HST. Despite his disappointment about being passed over for the top job, he set to and began the flagship development in express passenger train development in the UK. It was to be his last assignment.

The key to the success of the HST was the engine, this being a turbo-charged 12-cylinder 'V' high-speed diesel derived from the Paxman 'Ventura' unit. Of 2,250 horse-power each, the two engines per HST, one in each power car, gave a total of 4,500 hp for a train weight for an eight-coach set of 300 tons. Placing power cars at each end of the train simplified matters at termini, for with each power car having a driving compartment in the partially streamlined ends gave speedy turn-rounds with no light engine movements required.

Progress on the design was governed by the need to carry out some further analysis of the riding of the coaching stock and power car bogies. The recently designed class '86' electric locomotives had been proved satisfactory up to 100

Above: With speeds of 125 mph to be catered for, the locomotive windscreen needed to withstand the impact of foreign objects at that speed. Here Ron Jarvis and Bill Thorley (Traction Officer, BR HQ) examine the missile to be propelled against the test screen.   *Jarvis Collection*

Right: The rig being prepared for the high impact screen test.
                    Jarvis Collection

When Ron retired, he was presented with a Derby Porcelain figure by D.R. (Ron) Taylor, at that time the Assistant Director of Design (Traction). *J.B. Radford Collection*

Bodawen Lodge, Tremadoc, Ron and May's holiday home in Wales. *Jarvis Collection*

Production of HST power cars at Crewe works. By now Ron was retired and active on the Festiniog in Wales.   *Jarvis Collection*

A production HST set.   *Jarvis Collection*

mph, but the suspension design of that locomotive could not be used directly on the HST. The Research Department at Derby was therefore called into play and carried out a computer analysis of the riding characteristics. This indicated the way forward and, although not providing the final answer, at least permitted the first run of the prototype HST to be worked up to 125 mph, but on later trials problems occurred at 110 mph.

Subsequent modifications improved the riding qualities at the specified speeds and, eventually, a speed of 143 mph was safely achieved. This speed stood as a record for diesel traction for many years.

But this is taking us to the mid-1970s, by which time Ron was retired in Wales. The crucial design phase of the HST, which he was responsible for, laid the foundation for a very successful power unit which went into mass production and served reliably for many years on the BR main lines, only starting to become replaced in the early years of the 21st century.

The heavy spare time involvement on the Festiniog Railway, coupled to a great love of North Wales for holidays, led Ron and May to consider moving there once Ron had retired. His railway modelling was now on hold, having been displaced by the FR restoration and enhancement which reinforced his idea of spending much more time in the narrow gauge sphere.

Whilst ably fulfilling with his position at Derby, yet disappointed at the lack of perception by the BR top management in connection with locomotive developments, Ron began to think seriously about early retirement once the HST Prototype design had been completed. He would be 60 in 1971 and reached 43 years of service on the railways by then. His opinion of matters as they stood is clearly stated in a questionnaire circulated to all senior officers from the British Railways Board in April 1970, viz: 'Since I have been back in Derby 5 years no officer, senior to myself, has either had the time or taken the trouble to go round the drawing boards to find out what is involved in all the work going on', and, later on, when answering a question on the effectiveness of the existing BR organisation,

I would like to see significant changes. I have foreseen for nearly a decade and expressed this view to my superiors over and over again, that if we are going to have a railway in ten years time it is essential to develop new designs of locomotives and rolling stock, whilst our existing ones are still reasonably modern and satisfactory.

Eight to ten years is no excessive time in which to do this, with thoughtful planning and careful design, followed by prototype building, testing and service experience, and only after this to go into quantity production.

The financial system of BR does not appear to make this possible, e.g. no money may be spent on development until a project is authorised - this usually means that a locomotive is required for a specific duty in say two or three years. Only then is it authorised when it is far too late to develop the design and we have to botch up a 'new' locomotive using the designs of parts of older ones in conjunction with a few new details.

The engineer then tends to be criticised if the equipment does not come fully up to expectations.

Such outspoken comments indicated clearly that Ron missed the old days when the CME, such as Stanier, Ivatt and Riddles took a personal interest in the design matters under their remit, and saw to it that information was fed to the Board as required.

British Railways, with the HST, was to improve its express services considerably and attract quite a significant number of extra passengers back to rail travel as a result. Ron felt he would be happier in the restoration field, after all, his skills and patience there were much appreciated, more particularly since the previous year the bogie coach No. 16 had, at last, been fully restored. It had taken nine years in all to achieve that, but there was more to be done, and so, as his 60th birthday approached, Ron began making plans for retirement and a switch of home from Derby to Wales and of career from professional railway engineer to restorer of artifacts on a preserved narrow gauge line.

A further reason for early retirement was the discovery, following an operation in 1970, of the presence of diabetes. This, in the early days, could be satisfactorily treated with drugs and diet, which Ron meticulously controlled. However, as the years progressed, insulin had to be prescribed to control the condition. So long as he was able, this disability was not allowed to affect his restoration exercises for the FR.

Not long before he retired, Ron was alerted to the fact that the old Lancashire & Yorkshire dynamometer car No. 1 was listed for scrapping. This had been used extensively since it was constructed in 1912, and after 1923 the LMS had employed it on many important tests including those with the 'Royal Scot', also the non-stop Euston-Glasgow run with Stanier Pacific No. 6201 *Princess Elizabeth* in November 1936 and those with No. 6234 *Duchess of Abercorn* in 1939, the comparative tests of the locomotive exchanges of 1948 and subsequently some of the BR Standard steam locomotives, etc.

Brian Radford, then in the locomotive drawing office, had sent a letter to the Controller of Design and Development, D.R. Taylor, in the Railway Technical Centre requesting that this historic vehicle be made available for preservation as part of Derby Museum's Midland Railway Project. Ron, who we have seen, had been much involved in locomotive performance and testing by 1948, gave his whole-hearted support to this proposal and the BRB CME, T.C.B. Miller, agreed to the preservation and the car was saved. It is to be found today at the Midland Railway Centre, Butterley in Derbyshire.

Nearly 30 years on, this HST set leaves St Pancras for the Midlands.   *Author*

Chapter Twelve

Retirement and a Move to Wales

The opportunity to retire at 60 having been taken gladly by Ron meant that he could now apply much more time to Festiniog matters. The holiday home near Tremadog was used as a base and an exhaustive search around the nearby area for a retirement home commenced. They eventually found 'Llwyn-y-Pin', a former coach house near the village of Llanbedr. This property, set in about three acres of ground, included a driveway giving access through some woods to another house beyond. There were several outbuildings, of which the former stables appeared to offer potential for a sizeable workshop. This house was in a similar run-down condition as had been Bodawen Lodge and significant improvements and renovations were planned. Ron immediately spent some time on remedial work, such as renewing rotten barge-boards and replacing broken or loose slates. Their part of Bodawen Lodge was retained for the family to use as a holiday home.

Settling in at their new home, Ron and May initially spent a fair proportion of their time dealing with the grounds, tending the flower beds, planting and harvesting the vegetable garden and cutting the extensive lawns. Gradually their new home acquired a neat, fresh look and was to be their base for the rest of Ron's life. The stables were refurbished and turned into a workshop, being equipped with a fine circular saw and a planing machine in preparation for a further onslaught into the carriage restoration work.

Over the previous years of their frequent visits to this corner of Wales, many friends had been made, so it was easy to slip naturally into the life around Llanbedr village. The local church, St Peter's, was a first port-of-call and Ron was eventually to become its treasurer for some years, and an extremely competent one at that. May joined the local W.I. and was soon much involved in its affairs.

Some old memories were aroused in May 1975, when Stanier Pacific No. 46203 *Princess Margaret Rose* was being transferred by rail from Butlin's holiday camp at Pwllheli to Derby. This example of the first Pacific design of Stanier had stood as a static exhibit for 12 years and had been bought by the Midland Railway Company based at Butterley near Derby for eventual restoration to working order (this organisation has, for some time now, been known as the Midland Railway Trust (MRT)). The special train incorporating No. 46203 was scheduled to stop at nearby Barmouth station for a mechanical inspection before continuing its journey. Ron was alerted to this and made sure he was present to view this locomotive there on 11th May. Doubtless he was delighted to know that this example of Stanier's design expertise was going to be put back into service through the dedicated efforts of a group of enthusiasts. It was, initially, on loan from Butlin's, but eventually purchased outright by Brell Ewart, one of the MRT Directors, completely restored to working order and returned to main line service in 1990.

In addition to much spare time being devoted to the FR, Ron also became an active member of the Literary and Debating Society at Barmouth, and was quite often to give talks on a range of subjects, including railways, over the years. Always having strong Conservative views he joined the local Merioneth Conservative Association, and was to become its Chairman for some years. Integration into the life of that part of North Wales was assured.

On the coast near Llanbedr, were the sand dunes at Llandanwg. These were a local landmark, popular with both locals and holidaymakers, and had required some treatment to prevent erosion. The local authorities had spent considerable sums on their preservation. Behind the dunes nestled a small 15th century church, St Tanwg's, which was in a considerably run down state and in danger of becoming beyond repair. Ron and May frequently used to take walks in that area and noticed the condition of the Church. Ron decided that the preservation of this little building was important and offered his services to that end. This offer was gladly accepted by the Diocese and so he gave freely of his skills in its restoration and maintenance at a crucial time in the 1970s and thus ensured that the attractive little church continued to be a place of worship for those nearby, particularly when the holiday season boosted the population. Had this restoration not taken place, it would have quickly become a ruin and been lost forever.

Shortly after the preservation work had been completed the Prince of Wales visited Llandanwg to be shown the status of the sand dunes. Due to his efforts on the restoration of St Tanwg's Church there, Ron was included in the party which accompanied the Royal visitor.

With all the involvements around the local community, Ron never found time to settle down to writing an autobiographical account of his experiences, although he meticulously collected together a large amount of data to assist in this. It was the receipt of these personal archives that enabled the author to concoct this biography. Extensive archives such as these are often difficult, or impossible, to obtain at the best of times.

In 1978 Ron and May indulged themselves in a round-the-world trip. They had a good excuse for making this journey, as Rosemary, now happily married and with three children, was living in Papua New Guinea. Wishing to make the most of this long journey, they began by sailing to Sydney on the *Mikhail Lermontov*, a Russian ship. Departing from Southampton the sea trip took them across the Atlantic to Central America, through the Panama Canal and on across the Pacific Ocean, calling at Tahiti and Auckland on the way to Sydney. During the voyage across the Pacific, they crossed the Equator and watched the ceremony where King Neptune appeared to 'initiate' those crossing the line for the first time. Shortly after this they arrived at Tahiti, where a short trip ashore was made.

Leaving Tahiti, they sailed for Auckland and then on to Sydney, where a few days were spent taking the sights, before flying to Papua New Guinea to be reunited with Rosemary, her husband and the grandchildren for a three week stay.

All too soon the day of departure arrived and, flying to Manila, they caught an onward flight to Bangkok, where an eight day stay was made. The great sprawling city contained over five million inhabitants, the majority of whom lived in very run down, almost derelict, buildings, many of them built over water due to the proliferation of natural and man-made canals which abounded. The traffic, which was divided between water and road, produced a great contrast, with the slower boats noisily competing against the clamour of hooting road vehicles rushing through the streets.

Some of the 350 or so Buddhist temples in Bangkok were viewed and several trips out into the relative calm of the nearby smaller towns and villages were undertaken. Here they encountered a quieter life, with the natives mainly engaged in tending the extensive paddy fields with water buffalo as their motive power - the tractors of Thailand, as Ron so eloquently described them.

1978 was also the year in which Ron's elder brother, Geoffrey, died. He had taken over the family building business from their father and been its Managing Director for many years. To retain the family influence on the Board, Ron was elected as a Director. This gave him opportunities to visit Harpenden when Board Meetings were scheduled.

Although the railway modelling was but a past memory, there was a brief interlude when modelling returned. Ron and May constructed a model of a typical North Wales village, which included a section of the Festiniog Railway. This was displayed at the Welsh Fair in Builth Wells. Being quite bulky this model could not be stored at home and was placed under a stage at a local hall after its display. Unfortunately, it was subject to general deterioration and some vandalism which eventually put it beyond further use.

In the late spring of 1982 an official-looking envelope arrived in the post. It contained an invitation for Ron and May to attend a garden party at Buckingham Palace on 14th July. This was completely unexpected, but none the less they were delighted at the opportunity and gladly accepted the invitation. They stayed at Harpenden with Jim and Heather the night before the Garden Party, setting out from there in some trepidation, for the heavens had opened in a torrential downpour. They returned to recount their experiences and stay a further night before returning to Wales.

It had been back in the early 1970s that Ron was allotted the task of restoring the four remaining 4-wheeled carriages of 1863-4, known locally as 'Bug-boxes'. These veterans, built by Brown, Marshalls of Birmingham, were 10 ft long and 6 ft 3 in. wide and carried 12 to 14 passengers on back-to-back longitudinal seating. They dated almost from the inception of steam-hauled passenger trains on the FR, and had seen continuous service up to 1939. In 1959 the pressure of passenger business outstripped the rolling stock available and, at short notice, these vehicles had to be pressed into service. They then remained in traffic until their condition, due largely to the rotting of the main body members, made withdrawal inevitable for some of them. All sorts of patching up operations had been carried out over the years, with brackets and long nails, but the time had come to carry out a complete rebuilding.

It was possible to keep two of the four carriages for occasional use when rolling stock was at a premium, the other two being taken into the Boston Lodge works and stripped down for rebuilding. The underframes stayed in the works for repairing and modernising and Ron, at his workshop, began the long task of building completely new bodies. He worked as closely as possible to the original design, but some minor changes were made, primarily in the choice of

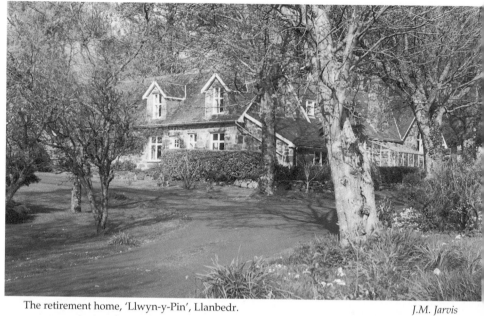

The retirement home, 'Llwyn-y-Pin', Llanbedr.   *J.M. Jarvis*

'Bug-box' No. 5 leaves 'Llwyn-y-Pin' for the FR Boston Lodge works, Portmadoc.   *J.M. Jarvis*

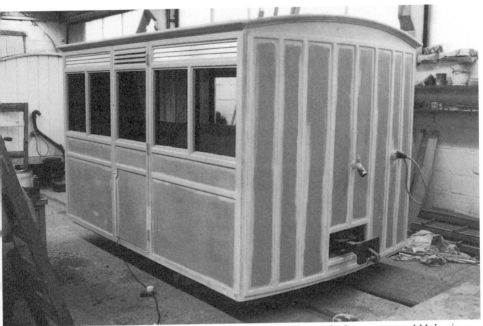

'Bug-box' No. 5 approaches completion in the FR works at Boston Lodge. *J.M. Jarvis*

The fruit of Ron's labours is ready for service. The restorer stands proudly by coach No. 5.
N. Gurley

ORIGINAL FESTINIOG BOGIE COACH (AS BUILT)

J.M. Jarvis

FR bogie coach No. 16 in service in 1970, a fitting tribute to Ron's handiwork.

more modern materials. The underframes, originally mainly wood, were rebuilt with steel members, which significantly strengthened the vehicle.

However, great attention was paid to ensuring that the general structure followed that of the original. Early railway carriages employed very similar methods in jointing to those used for coach-building techniques on horse-drawn road coaches so, on the dismantling, great care was taken to retain all the little pieces of rotting timber forming the mortises and tenons, then doing the jigsaw puzzle to reproduce the joint exactly as the craftsmen made it 120 years previously.

The first 'Bug-box' that Ron tackled was No. 5. The roof and sides were completely renewed but the curved end sections were retained as heavily repaired components. The sides were quite complex mouldings so Ron set to and had components made for all the extant 'Bug-boxes' being dealt with in this exercise. No 5 was completed after some years' work and he commenced on No. 6. This example had originally been a first class carriage and in about 1900 had been converted to an open observation car, probably due to deterioration of the upper sides. the decision was taken to rebuild this example as a first class closed carriage. Ron carefully laid aside the old side components with the idea that they could be used for a new open observation car in the future. Having started the rebuild, his general health began to fail and progress halted. The full life he had led since retirement, coupled to the approach of his eighties was beginning to have an effect on his capabilities. No. 6 was duly removed to Boston Lodge and completed there. Following Nos. 5 and 6, the remaining two, Nos. 3 and 4 were called into the works and rebuilt, using the components Ron had made when starting the project.

The end came gradually, commencing with a minor stroke in 1990. Recovery was partial, and a succession of more strokes occurred over the next few years. The cumulative effect of these strokes progressively destroyed his fine intellect and interests. The result was a gradual loss of his mental and physical powers, rather similar to the onset of Alzheimer's disease, but he was never categorised as having that affliction. However, despite this progressive illness, on his 80th birthday in 1991, he was able to participate in the celebration organised by the family for that event. Jim had prepared a 'This is Your Life' red book chronicling Ron's life and career which was presented to him with due ceremony.

By 1993 he was virtually helpless much of the time, which put an incredible strain on May. Their many good friends rallied round, helping as they could, to assist May in her endeavour to give Ron the best attention she could.

He was clearly frustrated at not being able to carry out many of the normal tasks of life, but retained a remarkably calm and patient appearance. The carriage restoration tasks under way at the time of the commencement of his disability were being dealt with by other volunteers, with the partly completed bodies which had been transferred from his workshop at 'Llwyn-y-Pin' to the Boston Lodge works of the FR.

By the middle of 1994 his health was even more on the decline and he was admitted to Llandudno Hospital in the late summer. He died peacefully on the 2nd September of that year. He would have been 83 the following November.

St Peter's Church, Llanbedr. The interior had a lot of remedial work carried out by Ron over many years.   *J.M. Jarvis*

St Tanwg's Church, behind the sand dunes at Llandanwg near Harlech. Ron played an important part in the restoration of this small building. Periodic services were then held in it with a fair/good attendance.   *J.M. Jarvis*

Paddington 4th December, 1994. Rebuilt 'Merchant Navy' class No. 35028 *Clan Line* at Paddington on a steam special. That particular weekend the locomotive carried Ron's name. Note the other Ron Jarvis design in the form of an HST in platform 4.   *J.M. Jarvis*

The funeral service was held at St Peter's Church, Llanbedr, conducted by his good friend Canon Stephen Beck, followed by the burial in the churchyard outside. Canon Beck gave an address which spoke eloquently about Ron's life, his involvement in matters locally and as a person.

In his will, Ron bequeathed to the FR his workshop equipment in the shape of the circular saw and planing machine, which were installed in the Boston Lodge works, and are still much in use. His magnificent collection of railway negatives, before his death, was donated to the Midland Railway Trust at Butterley, which holds their copyright, and is now organised to market prints from them.

So ended a long and full life with railways very much to the fore, a life which had encompassed involvement in the steam locomotive for the final decades of its development, followed by extensive work on electric, electro-diesel and diesel-electric locomotives and, finally, the HST, this latter still with us today as a major provider of express travel.

Amongst the many letters of condolence to be sent to May was perhaps, the best accolade Ron could have received for his professional career. This stated that he was, 'the finest practical locomotive engineer' that he had come across.

Not long after Ron's death, some kind of memorial to him on the railways was suggested as being appropriate. This was to take the form of one of the power cars of an HST set being named 'Ronald G. Jarvis' in recognition of his design work that led up to the most successful fleet of express passenger trains to run on British railways. Unfortunately, due to circumstances at the time, the intended naming and associated ceremony never took place.

May continued to live in Llanbedr until 1996, when she was persuaded to leave and go to live near Rosemary who, by then, was settled in Exeter. She passed away in Exmouth in August 1999 at the fine age of 94.

Appendix One

Delivering Locomotives to Turkey

A broadcast made by Ron Jarvis on the BBC Home Service, Tuesday 15th December, 1942

The British Government look upon Turkey as a firm friend and as such we've got to help her in every way we can: that's why it was decided about a couple of years ago to send a number of locomotives and wagons out to Turkey, at some sacrifice to ourselves considering the need we have for locomotives in this country.

Well, actually 18 locomotives were sent out and over 500 twenty-ton wagons: they commenced shipment about a year last February. There were two of us from the LMS Railway detailed to go out, because the locomotives were of LMS design and we had to superintend the erection of this stock, get it running and instruct the Turkish railway staff in working it. The gauge in Turkey is exactly the same as we have here and that means British railway stock can perfectly well run on Turkish railways. Turkey is a very mountainous country: practically every section of the railway traverses mountains. As for conditions - you have extreme heat and dustiness in summer-time and, in many parts of the country, extreme cold in winter-time. That is to say, at Ankara in the summer it's about 100 degrees in the shade and during last winter where we were it was down to 63 degrees of frost - about 30 below. So that during winter you get conditions of extreme frost with a large amount of snow up in the mountain sections, and it's quite a frequent occurrence for trains to get snowed up, despite the use of rotary snow ploughs.

We arrived in Turkey about May of 1941 and that was at a time when Turkey was surrounded by the war without being in it. The Greek Campaign was over to all intents and purposes - actually our forces were just out of Greece - we were being turned out of Crete; Iraq was still in turmoil. There were beginning to be rumours about Persia being infiltrated; the Russian position was uncertain; Syria was in the hands of Vichy and the Germans had started to use Syrian aerodromes, and of course there was, at that time, quite a considerable threat to Egypt, so Turkey was very nearly ringed by our enemies - Bulgaria and Roumania having been taken over by the Nazis. Well, we went to Turkey and when we arrived it wasn't without some mixed feelings as to what we were walking into, and we were very relieved to find at least the Turks, while realising the seriousness of the position, were still sure we were going to win.

I'd better explain that the type of engine sent was a 2-8-0 which in this country is used purely on freight services. In Turkey, where passenger train speeds are considerably lower, the same locomotive becomes a maid-of-all-work. It's used on passenger trains, freight trains or, as the majority of trains are, a combination of both.

Now the position as regards getting our material to Turkey was that, owing to the collapse of Greece and the occupation of the Greek Islands off the coast of Turkey it was at any rate inadvisable for our ships to go to the big ports of Turkey, and consequently the only ports that were available were those two right in the corner of Asia Minor - almost the top right-hand corner of the Mediterranean - Iskenderun better known as Alexandretta, and Mersin. And neither of them was too well equipped to deal with heavy loads.

We set to work, first of all, to make arrangements which would enable our cargoes of railway material to be off-loaded principally at Iskendenrun.

For reasons of shipping, most of our earlier shipments were off-loaded far away in Egypt. It was not until September that anything came through for us in Turkey, but meanwhile by pegging away at Iskenderun we got the crane rigged up, more railway lines laid, other cranes repaired; in fact, quite a reorganisation of the port was in hand.

The locomotives were shipped dismantled. The boiler went in one piece and so did the underframe complete with cylinders. These were the heavy lifts. The rest consisted of a tender tank, a tender frame and eight pairs of wheels. The small parts were packed in 11 packing cases for each locomotive.

The actual job of erecting the locomotive was carried out at Sivas - a very ancient town, I believe at one time the capital of Eastern Anatolia. It lies a little to the north-east of the centre of Asiatic Turkey and is about 4,000 feet up in the mountains.

Sivas is a real old-fashioned place quite like you see in films of mediaeval England. The streets are roughly paved, and the houses built of timber and white-washed mud-bricks have a tumbledown appearance. Until about 10 years ago, when the railway opened to Sivas, the town had little connection with the outside world. The extension of the railway beyond Sivas to the east was only recently carried out.

There are about 40,000 inhabitants, who are mostly peasant farmers. But the railway workshops situated there are very up-to-date and employ about 2,000 men. We found the Turks very friendly. They gave us every assistance and we had good relations with them all the time.

All the time we were quite on our own. Incidentally, we were probably among the first Englishmen ever to live at Sivas. We were in a rather unusual position in that we hadn't any men of our own working for us. We were only there in an advisory capacity and we had to persuade rather than give orders. In this way we succeeded in keeping the workmen hard at it, but nevertheless we kept on extremely good terms the whole time, and when the first locomotive went to Ankara for inspection, we were told there that it was the quickest job that had ever been done in Turkey.

We had many amusing experiences and sometimes they were a bit alarming. A good example was the moment the first engine was finished. Before we had had a chance to test her, the Turks were so anxious to get her running that they filled her up with water, put a fire in and drove her out on the first trial run before even the brakes had been tested, and the speed at which they took the curves on this occasion was quite alarming. But she did all right, and there wasn't the slightest trouble as a result of it, although of course the initial running should be carried out at a reasonable speed to see that nothing runs hot. The thing was that they put the engine through her paces and the paces were a bit excessive for our peace of mind.

Then the next trip she did was from Sivas right across the mountains to a junction in the East - a matter of 65 miles away - and she hauled a heavy freight train of 400 tons. My colleague was on the footplate on this particular occasion - I didn't go. Now the coal supplied was not too good according to our standards and it was a bit difficult to keep up steam: but anyway, she worked the train all right that day, and the day afterwards the paintwork was finished off and the following day she was sent off at the head of the express to Ankara, 375 miles away, which she did in about 19 hours. Of course, the country is very mountainous and an assisting engine was attached for negotiating the steep inclines, as is usual with heavy trains. During part of this run I had a very interesting time on the footplate.

At Ankara the engine was much admired because she was so neat and shapely in contrast to the engines of German design - quite a little piece of England in Turkey - or a piece of Britain I suppose I should say, because she was made in Scotland. She worked back to Sivas and then we had to take her in hand and alter the blast arrangements in order to burn the Turkish coal, and after slight modifications she was perfectly satisfactory.

By this time the second engine was already finished and three more were in hand.

There was a lot of delay actually in getting these locomotive parts through to us: this was partly on account of shipping difficulties and then later when the winter came along it was the worst winter in Turkey for over 50 years - and the Anatolian Highlands are well known for being a cold spot! The railways themselves were closed almost continuously

166 RON JARVIS : FROM MIDLAND COMPOUND TO THE HST

during January and February; on the mountain sections, where there were great snow drifts, and though rotary snow ploughs were in use, as soon as they had swept the line and before a train could move up, the wind had blown the snow back on to the track again.

Despite all this, the locomotives and wagons were delivered and set to work in Turkey. That Great Britain could, at so critical a stage in the war, implement her promises to Turkey in the face of the worst our enemies could do, was to say the least, a very creditable achievement.

We left in May, when 16 of the locomotives were in service and the remaining two were being completed.

There were about 430 out of 500 wagons finished and the remainder could easily be dealt with by the Turks as they arrived.

What it comes to is that to Turkey and to various other countries in that direction such as Persia and Egypt and Syria, we have parted with a number of our biggest freight locomotives, and this has been a considerable sacrifice to us and we've got a good deal of work to do to replace these locomotives, considering our needs in this war. There's no doubt that these locomotives will help the Turks and in my opinion, it's worth the sacrifice we have made. I do hope also that the locomotives and wagons will give a good account of themselves so that it will lead in the post-war period to increased trade and thereby increased friendship and closer ties between our two countries.

Although the engines we have parted with were freight and not passenger locomotives, the effect is that a certain number of engines that would normally be used for passenger traffic have had to be put on freight trains. And that, of course, has had its repercussions on the passenger services which the railway companies can run in this country until those sacrifices that we have made in this was are made good by new building. This is one of the reasons why you, as a traveller, may be experiencing some discomfort and annoyance at the moment.

Appendix Two

The Franco-Crosti Boiler

The following description of the principles of the Franco-Crosti boiler has been taken from the Brighton Memorandum ref. TL8/7/2 issued on 6th July, 1951 by Ron Jarvis following his visit to Germany to inspect the type 52 locomotives so modified.

The boiler itself is of substantially normal design, but the flue gases, instead of escaping from the smokebox by way of the normal chimney, are conducted through a passage in the smokebox door to a lower and separate compartment of the smokebox. From here they pass through the tubes of the two pre-heater drums, placed under the boiler barrel and slightly inclined to the rear. Small smoke boxes are provided at the back end of the preheaters and a chimney emerges on either side of the boiler just forward of the front of the firebox. The exhaust steam from the cylinders passes to a jacket surrounding part of the pre-heaters and then passes to a group of three small blast pipes located at the base of each chimney. The normal chimney at the front end of the engine is fitted with a shutter and this is opened for the chimney to be used only during lighting up.

The pre-heaters are fed by injectors or feed pumps and contain water at boiler pressure. A pipe from the front end conducts the feed water to a top feed clack on the boiler proper.

The object is to improve the thermal efficiency of the locomotive in the following respects:

(i)   The lowering of the temperature of the exhaust gases to the greatest practicable extent.

(ii)   The abstraction of some heat from the exhaust steam.

(iii)   The use of higher superheats, made possible by the separation of the superheater from the escaping flue gases. The boiler proper is so tubed that the intermediate smokebox gases are appreciably hotter than would be permissible in a normal locomotive, the additional heat in the gases being abstracted subsequently in the pre-heaters.

(iv)   By keeping the resistance low in both boiler and pre-heaters, no excessive blast is called for. The fact of cooling the gases to a lower temperature, and the benevolent circle of events, lead to reduction in both weight and volume of the flue gases to be exhausted. The pull on the fire is assisted by the contraction of the gases which takes place.

(v)   The benevolent circle of events, which increases the efficiency and therefore reduces the coal burned for a given power. This means, in general, an improved grate efficiency resulting from a lower rate of firing.

A Crosti boiler, this type with a reverse flow which results in the exhaust being at the front, destined for a NORTE locomotive. This photograph was sent to Ron by Professor Crosti himself. *Jarvis Collection*

Appendix Three

Facts and Figures for Bulleid Pacifics

This Appendix has been drawn from examination of Ron Jarvis' analysis and subsequent reports/papers concerning the necessity of rebuilding the popular but temperamental and troublesome Bulleid Pacifics.

The three main express locomotives on the Southern Region of BR were compared in terms of the yearly number of weekdays out of traffic for running repairs and examinations per engine, and gave the following results:

'Merchant Navy'	62
'West Country'	54
'Lord Nelson'	39

In 1953, considering the 'Merchant Navy' and 'West Country' classes, engine defects at sheds accounted for the loss of 5,500 days for the 140 locomotives, averaging 39 days per engine, with the following individual causes standing out:

Valve gear	1,021 days
Valves and pistons	251 days
Steam and exhaust pipes	423 days
Grates and ashpans	215 days
Steam reverser	50 days

Clearly, something had to be done about the valve gear and the steam and exhaust pipes, which constituted some 75 per cent of the above causes.

In terms of repair costs per mile the following figures were gathered:

'Merchant Navy'	13.7d.
'West Country'	11.9d.
'Lord Nelson'	10.7d.
Other Regions' Pacifics	8.9d.

The 'Lord Nelson', apart from being four-cylindered, were over 20 years old and becoming somewhat worn. The Gresley and Stanier Pacifics which constituted those of the other Regions show up particularly well, despite the problems inherent with the conjugated gear and middle big end of the former.

As regards the cost of general and intermediate repairs of the Bulleid Pacifics, these were some £650 (£20,000 today) per annum greater than that for a 'Lord Nelson'. This was largely due to the expense of removing, repairing and replacing the air-smoothed casing and repairing the valve gear and associated parts.

In terms of coal and water consumption, some comparison with the BR class '7' Pacific indicated a value, in terms of lb. per dbhp hour of +11 per cent for the 'Merchant Navy' and a corresponding water increase of +12 per cent. This was bad enough, but when comparing oil consumption the amount required per locomotive every 100 miles was 15 pints for the 'Merchant Navy', to which had to be added a further 16 pints for loss due to leakage from the oil bath. A total of 31 pints per 100 miles. The corresponding amount required for the 'Lord Nelson' was 9½ pints per 100 miles. The three-fold increase in high quality expensive lubricating oil clearly could not be tolerated.

No. 35014 *Nederland Line.*   *Jarvis Collection*

Based on the above figures some conservative conclusions were applied in estimating the cost savings of modifying the 140 locomotives to incorporate improvements to bring them into line with other comparable, engines. The Regional Accountant estimated that the expenditure required to modify the fleet would be recouped in reduced maintenance and operating costs in about seven years. In fact, for the 90 engines rebuilt, the total cost was recouped in just four years and Bulleid's design lived on to see the end of steam on the Southern Region. So popular did the original and modified designs become that no fewer than 24, of both types, have been preserved, demonstrating the engineering expertise of Ron Jarvis well into the 21st century.

A close-up of the new outside valve gear which replaced the original chain-driven inside arrangement.   *Jarvis Collection*

Appendix Four

The Festiniog Railway

The Festiniog Railway in North Wales was built to bring down the slate from the quarries at Blaenau Ffestiniog to the sea at Portmadoc, from where it could be shipped to all parts of the World.

The railway, 13 miles long, was opened in 1836 and, initially, employed gravity as the means of propulsion of the loaded trains. This was made possible by the fact that there was a falling gradient all the way from the quarries to the sea. Horses were used to haul the empty wagons back, and for the down trip they rode in a specially designed wagon.

In 1863 steam locomotives were acquired and these took over the work of the horses, but the slate trains were still operated by gravity until well into the 20th century. The design of locomotives for so narrow a gauge as 60 cm (approximately 2 ft) presented difficulties at that time, but they were successful and, indeed, the two original locomotives are still in existence.

With the introduction of locomotives the possibility existed of introducing a passenger service and, for this purpose, a batch of four-wheeled carriages was ordered from the Birmingham coach building firm of Brown, Marshall. These were supplied in 1864 and were probably the first narrow-gauge passenger carriages in the World. They were very unusual inasmuch as the seating was longitudinal and back-to-back - in fact they were like park seats with wheels and running gear installed inside, and with a box-like body over the top.

The railway continued to carry passengers right up to the outbreak of war in 1939 and the ever-lessening amount of slate until 1946, when it closed down completely. In 1954, however, the railway was taken over by a band of enthusiasts who revitalised the whole undertaking, and contrary to the predictions of most people at the time, have made the subsequent history of the company a success story of no mean proportions. Of freight there is none, but the passenger services have now been re-introduced all the way from Portmadoc to Blaenau Ffestiniog.

The Festiniog was to become famous in railway circles for two unique developments associated with it, these being, firstly the introduction of the bogie passenger carriage in the UK and, secondly, the employment of articulated locomotives. The bogie carriages were designed by George Percy Spooner (1850-1916) in 1871 of which Nos. 15 and 16 still exist, the latter having been completely restored by Ron Jarvis.

The articulated locomotive was introduced by Robert Fairlie (1831-1885) who, in 1864, patented a double-ended all-adhesion locomotive mounted on two powered bogies. His first prototype was built for the 2 ft gauge and carried out its trials on the Festiniog Railway in 1869. It was so successful that articulated steam locomotives were adopted elsewhere and, to this day, the Festiniog employs a Fairlie locomotive.

Appendix Five

Preserved BR Standard Locomotives designed under Ron Jarvis

Class	Type	No.	Withdrawn	Built at	Now found at
4	4-6-0	75014	1966	Swindon	North Yorks Moors Railway
		75027	1968	Swindon	Bluebell Railway
		75029	1967	Swindon	North Yorks Moors Railway
		75069	1967	Swindon	Severn Valley Railway
		75078	1966	Swindon	Keighley & Worth Valley Railway
		75079	1966	Swindon	Plym Valley Railway
4	2-6-4T	80002	1967	Brighton	Keighley & Worth Valley Railway
		80064	1965	Brighton	Bluebell Railway
		80072	1965	Brighton	Llangollen Railway
		80078	1965	Brighton	Swanage Railway
		80079	1965	Brighton	Severn Valley Railway
		80080	1965	Brighton	Midland Railway Centre
		80097	1965	Brighton	East Lancs Railway
		80098	1965	Brighton	Churnet Valley Railway
		80100	1965	Brighton	Bluebell Railway
		80104	1965	Brighton	Swanage Railway
		80105	1965	Brighton	Bo'ness & Kinneil Railway
		80135	1965	Brighton	North Yorks Moors Railway
		80136	1965	Brighton	West Somerset Railway
		80150	1965	Brighton	Vale of Glamorgan Railway
		80151	1965	Brighton	Bluebell Railway
9	2-10-0	92134	1966	Crewe	Railway Age, Crewe
		92203	1967	Swindon	Swindon Railway Workshop, Bream
		92207	1964	Swindon	East Lancs Railway
		92212	1968	Swindon	Mid-Hants Railway
		92214	1965	Swindon	Midland Railway Centre
		92219	1965	Swindon	Midland Railway Centre
		*92220	1965	Swindon	NRM
		92240	1965	Crewe	Bluebell Railway
		92245	1964	Crewe	Vale of Glamorgan Railway

Notes

All the tanks were withdrawn more or less at the same time as diesel mutiple units took over the passenger work normally allocated to them.

All 2-10-0s after No. 92203 have double chimneys.

*The last steam locomotive built by BR, *Evening Star*.

Appendix Six

The Funeral Address
Given by Canon Stephen Beck MA

Ronald Guy Jarvis
R.I.P.
St Peter's Church, Llanbedr
Friday, September 9th, 1994 at 2.00 pm

We are met today in the shadow of loss. We are here to share our sorrow, and to show our sympathy. We have come to bid farewell to a friend, and a dear relation, to commit his tired body to the good earth, and to commend his deathless spirit to the God and Father of us all who gave it; to pay our tribute of love and regard to one who has travelled the road of life with us, and who has gone on ahead. We shall follow in God's good time. To pay tribute - yes - and to pray for him. He needs our prayers just as we need his. For we are members of one family, and all members of separated families need each other's prayers. Such partings as this mean sorrow, God knows - and indeed God does know. He knows because Jesus Our Lord Himself was not ashamed to show His grief at the graveside of a friend, his dear friend Lazarus, when we are told that 'Jesus wept', and we may hold on to the knowledge that our sorrow is, so to say, the reverse side of the love that we feel, and therefore most of us would not wish it to be other than it is.

But a little later, St John records that 'Jesus gave thanks' - and so do we - sorrow mingled with thanksgiving - a fact of life. So for us today, our grief and our gratitude are not ill-blended. We give thanks to God for a life lived to the full, devoted, enthusiastic, conscientious, whole-hearted, and of that life most of you will have your special memories to clothe my words with life.

Today I am the diffident spokesman for a wealth of memory represented by your combined presence here in this church, and, hopefully, sustained by the prayers and thoughts of many more who cannot be.

I have not found it easy - it never is - and it grows harder with the years - to frame our farewell to Ron. There is no time, maybe there is no need, for me to speak at length of his boyhood in Harpenden, suffice to say his home and surroundings were ideal and fulfilling ones in which to grow up. It was a happy childhood, and even then the seeds were sown of his single-minded pursuit of engineering as a career, and his passion for railway engines goes without saying. Even as a very small boy on holiday, he recalls watching them in the railway yard below from the upper windows of the house where he stayed near Barmouth front in those early days. Building models, photographing ancient engines in all sorts of places, engrossed him. He left school early, at 15, to his headmaster's disapproval, but Ron knew what he was about, even at that tender age, and pursued an apprenticeship in Derby in the late 20s, in the course of which he also gained an external Honours Degree in Engineering from London. Railway engines were his life, and he was building up his skill and experience from the late 20s in Derby, right through to the War years, when in the early 40s he was responsible for supervising the assembly of a large consignment of railway engines which had been shipped to Turkey, ending the War years with an assignment of great interest in India.

All this was preparation for the main part of his career spent in Derby and Brighton and back again, ending up as a distinguished locomotive design engineer, from which he took an earlyish retirement at 60; and it was to here that he and May came to 'retire'. For his retirement, at the height of his powers in the early 70s represented a quarter of a lifetime still ahead; and so a substantial part of their married life of 52 years has been spent here amongst us.

All through his life he was a home-maker, loving his home and his family, and he not only had an instinct and enthusiasm for this, but also the capacity and talents to carry out his plans; and so it was natural that he should provide himself with a workshop when he reached his Llanbedr home, upon which he effected such a dramatic transformation. And the knowledge and experience acquired in his Railway career was able to be lavished on the Festiniog Railway which he had also become involved with in earlier days in Derby and Brighton, long before retirement. '*Si monumentum requiris circumspice*' - that Latin tag reflects the wonderful work he did in building and restoration which caused the Festiniog Railway three years ago to honour his achievements and record their gratitude.

Two church friends of his have both spoken to me recently almost with awe, certainly with immense respect and admiration, of his extraordinary skills and precision in restoration in wood. How did he do it? A gift from God? Be sure that nothing was too much trouble. Nor could anybody hurry him in his pursuit of perfection.

Ron and May together quickly became highly involved in the community they had come in to. I do not need to refer to Ron's affection for Llanbedr Church, and what could be more fitting than that we should be saying farewell to him here, where he will rest, in St Peter's Churchyard. He has served this Church with great faithfulness and was for many years, as his character would lead you to expect, a meticulous church treasurer. Nor should I forget to mention St Tanwgs among the Sand Dunes in nearby Llandanwg. He was very fond of it. He gave freely of his skills in its maintenance and restoration at a vital time in the 70s, when , without his care and enthusiasm, that beautiful building and its worship might well have lost the battle for survival.

And then there was Ronald Guy Jarvis the man - his birthday - November 5th - explains his second name. He was a good man, a gentleman in the literal sense. A good all-rounder - as such interests as Probus, his characteristically and conscientiously active erstwhile chairmanship of the Merioneth Conservative Association, his support of the Arts and the local Literary and Debating Society, and his service and wise council to the diocese, and all the other things I've mentioned will testify.

There was about him always a certain simplicity and youthfulness even in old age. He'd a boyish sense of humour, too. He was a kind man. And courteous. Someone said to me recently - 'He treated you at the time as though you were the one person he wanted to be with at that moment'. He was kind and also very generous; and there will be many who will be grateful for his capacity to help people, and always in the most unobtrusive way. His kindness was by stealth.

For all that and much else besides that the time would fail me to tell of, and for all our memories of this good man, we bless him and give God thanks today. But we are Christ's men and women and this is a service, not only of sorrow and thanksgiving and remembrance, but also of hope. We say our goodbye - which means 'God be with you' - to our dear Ron in the faith and trust that Christ died and rose again for us. He is alive and with us still. We share in His Resurrection and Strange Victory. Death becomes through Him not a terminus but a thoroughfare - a Road to God. And it is in that Hope - strong word - no vague hoping for the best - it is in that Hope that we entrust our friend and loved one, faithfully, hopefully, lovingly to the God-and-Father - who fully understands him, and accepts him - in whose nearer presence he will no longer see thro' a glass darkly but face to face, who will give him as, please God, He will give us all, peace, enlightenment and reassurance, joy and, surely, endless opportunities of further service.

May he rest in that peace,

Amen.

Bibliography

Application of Diesel Engines to Rail Traction by T. Hornbuckle, DEUA, 1936.
Barry Scrapyard by Alan Warren, Guild Publishing.
BRB files of Reports and Memoranda (Brighton 1950-64), Ron Jarvis Collection.
British Locomotives of the 20th Century by O.S. Nock, Patrick Stephens Ltd.
British Railways Standard Steam Locomotives by R.C. Bond, Ian Allan.
Derby Works and Midland Locomotives by J.B. Radford, Ian Allan.
Journal of the Stephenson Locomotive Society, various.
LMS 150 by Patrick Whitehouse and David St John Thomas, David & Charles.
Proceedings, the Institution of Mechanical Engineers.
Rail Centres: Brighton by B.K. Cooper, Ian Allan.
Reports and Memoranda from Turkey 1941-2, Ron Jarvis Collection.
Riddles and the 9Fs by Col H.C.B. Rogers, Ian Allan.
Ron Jarvis, letters from Turkey and India.
Royal Air Force 1939-45, Volume 1 by Denis Richards, HMSO.
Sir William Stanier - a new biography by J.E. Chacksfield, The Oakwood Press.
Steam from Waterloo by Col H.C.B. Rogers, David & Charles.
The Application of Diesel Engines to Rail Traction by T. Hornbuckle, Diesel
    Engine Users Association, ref. S.133.
T. Hornbuckle, letters to Ron Jarvis, 1939-58.
The Oxford Companion to British Railway History edited by Jack Simmons and
    Gordon Biddle, Oxford University Press.
The Railway Gazette, various.
The Rebuilding of the Bulleid Pacifics by R.G. Jarvis, paper given in 1976 to
    the MNLPS.
The Second World War by Winston S. Churchill, Cassell & Co. Ltd.

Ron's grave in the churchyard of St Peter's, Llanbedr. May standing nearby.   *J.M. Jarvis*

Index

Numbers in **bold** type refer to illustrations.